T0196094

Also by Jane Bryan

Project Leadership

Coming Soon:
Biography: The Book of Laura

Coming Soon: Travel Books
Our Travels in Spain
Scotland
Ireland
Our Awesome Travels in Italy

THE LEADER IN ME

Success Strategies for Project Leadership

JANE BRYAN

BALBOA.
PRESS

A DIVISION OF HAY HOUSE

Balboa Press books may be ordered through booksellers or by contacting:

Balboa Press
A Division of Hay House
1663 Liberty Drive
Bloomington, IN 47403
www.balboapress.com
1 (877) 407-4847

Because of the dynamic nature of the Internet, any web addresses or links contained in this book may have changed since publication and may no longer be valid. The views expressed in this work are solely those of the author and do not necessarily reflect the views of the publisher, and the publisher hereby disclaims any responsibility for them.

The author of this book does not dispense medical advice or prescribe the use of any technique as a form of treatment for physical, emotional, or medical problems without the advice of a physician, either directly or indirectly. The intent of the author is only to offer information of a general nature to help you in your quest for emotional and spiritual well-being. In the event you use any of the information in this book for yourself, which is your constitutional right, the author and the publisher assume no responsibility for your actions.

Any people depicted in stock imagery provided by Getty Images are models, and such images are being used for illustrative purposes only. Certain stock imagery © Getty Images.

Print information available on the last page.

ISBN: 978-1-9822-1953-6 (sc)
ISBN: 978-1-9822-1955-0 (hc)
ISBN: 978-1-9822-1954-3 (e)

Library of Congress Control Number: 2019900233

Balboa Press rev. date: 01/15/2019

Preface

THIS SHORT COMPREHENSIVE workbook on leading projects provides on-the-job practices that help you expand your leadership skills. You will learn how to build a foundation for success, develop amazing, high-productive teams, deliver project success, and celebrate success. You will learn how to become a partner with the project sponsor, how to practice good communication with your team, and how to have a rock-solid risk mitigation process. The skills you'll learn and practice in this book are taught within the context of project management. However, these skills can be used in any career and will provide the type of life you desire and deserve and will help you prosper.

Jane Bryan also provides consulting services on the information covered in this book. She loves connecting with clients via social media. You can find her at www.linkedin.com/in/jane-bryan-4731351 or janebryan601@gmail.com.

Contents

Introduction

Project Leadership

WHILE WORKING IN management and project management, I observed that some leadership practices almost always led to success, but if these practices were skipped, they often resulted in disappointing outcomes. These were not elusive skills that only a few could learn but skills and practices everyone can develop quickly on the job and use to substantially improve their career and family life.

You have the potential to develop the leader in you. True leadership stems from learned skills, and anyone can do so with the right on-the-job training and experience. Leadership is not just a position you hold but how you conduct yourself. Making the choice to develop the leader in you will impact every aspect of your life. A leader works with others to achieve a vision or goal.

This book is designed to help you develop project leadership skills and practices. As a project leader, you

- Use your leadership skills with the sponsor, stakeholders, and your team to lead them to success;
- Create focused, energized teams to reach peak levels of productivity;
- Find amazing opportunities that you never thought possible; and
- Create wealth for yourself and your family.

My goal is to help you recognize and affirm your unique leadership skills and knowledge, your potential, and your ability to expand into what makes you extraordinary. Take action and verify your greatness, as it will benefit and enhance the lives of everyone you work with. For example, by building high-performing teams, not only will it benefit you, but each team member will be energized and open to new ideas. If you are able to form strong partnerships with your project sponsor (a manager or executive with accountability to deliver the project vision, governance, and agreed-upon business benefits for the organization) and resolve any issues with the project, you will be viewed as someone who can move to other opportunities while your sponsor will trust you, value your skills, and support you.

Expanding your leadership skills enhances your ability to have a thriving career. The skills I discuss have brought me much success.

Leadership is one of the most important skills in project management. The four phases of project management involve leadership skills and practices that, in combination, can bring you amazing success. Leadership begins as soon as the project is assigned to you. There is a strong relationship between your leadership and your team's performance. As you spend time developing your leadership skills and continue to grow, your teams are also growing and becoming extraordinary. The synergy between you and your team will lead you to amazing success. If you immediately establish yourself as the leader, you will find the overall project enjoyable and energizing for your team.

This book focuses on the leadership skills and practices needed at each of the four phases of project management. Below is a brief summary of the importance of each phase, which has an entire chapter devoted to each leadership skill and practice.

Chapter 1 is project initiation, or building a foundation for success. Leadership skills and practices are described to help you become a leader to the sponsor, stakeholders, and team members through communication and the importance of forming strong partnerships. Leadership and good communication are tools needed to successfully complete a project.

Chapter 2 is planning the project or creating amazing teams. Leadership skills and practices to help you build a highly productive team are discussed. The focus is on specific ways to build your role as a leader. If you are unsuccessful in developing your leadership role during project initiation and planning, it is almost impossible to deliver the business results. Both initiating and planning the project are time intensive but pay amazing dividends. In some organizations there is a tendency to skip these two phases and jump right into the work of the project. Not only will the project have less chance of success, but you may not be viewed as a leader. In these situations, each team member often works independently without a strong sense of team or commitment to the project.

Chapter 3 is about delivering project success, which builds on initiation and planning. The leadership skills and practices you have followed while planning and executing the project will enable you to achieve success. For example, if the project did not include planning but jumped immediately into completing tasks, risks have not been identified, and a risk mitigation process is not in place. The risks and problems continue to build during the project until there is such a mountain of problems that it is almost impossible to resolve them. The reason this occurs is that everyone is working independently and may not recognize the risks or thinks it is everyone else's responsibility to solve them.

Chapter 4, project close or celebrating success, is the end result of a successful project. You will now be viewed as a leader in your organization. This chapter focuses on tools you can use to share the team successes with other leaders and let them know you welcome new and different opportunities. For example, if you have led your team in a new and innovative approach that enhances the business goals of your organization, you will be viewed as a leader with vision.

Career Growth Opportunities

You have a bright future ahead as a professional project leader. Skilled project leaders are in demand in the global market. Let's look at some research conducted by the Project Management Institute (PMI), the premier organization for project management in the United States. In 2017 it published research titled "Job Growth and Talent Gap 2017–27." They found that there are currently not enough project professionals to meet the demand in many countries, including China, India, United States, Brazil, Japan, Great Britain, Canada, Australia, and other countries. Their research shows that demand will continue to increase over the next decade.

Their research shows that an amazing 97 percent of organizations believe project management is critical to business performance and organizational success. They predict there will be fifteen million new high-level project management jobs for people with leadership, communication, and technical knowledge of project management and business. They predict this trend will continue until 2027.

The study also indicated that the demand for project professionals was growing faster than the demand in other occupations. The analysis indicated that worldwide, project-related jobs would reach around 52.4 million by 2020. They estimated that 2.2 million new project roles will be created each year through 2027.

Increased demand for leaders who are project professionals is occurring for three reasons. First, organizations are increasingly using project management practices that result in more opportunities. Using advances in technology and project management practices help organizations successfully complete projects. The main reason for this increase in the use of project management practices is closely related to the next reason.

Second, the ongoing explosion in technology has revitalized projects, enhancing information sharing, problem solving, instant communications, cost management, change management, and other factors. Constantly updating your technology skills to remain current is essential.

Third, current project professionals with leadership skills are reaching retirement age, opening the field to new talent. If you have the right set of skills, including leadership and communication, and are current with technology, you have an extremely positive job outlook. A challenge you will face is that many of these jobs may not be in your current geographic location. You may have to look for work further afield. I experienced this in my career. My best opportunities involved weekly travel. I frequently traveled, leaving home on Sunday and returning on Friday evening. Traveling or working remotely need to be considered.

Path to Becoming a Professional Project Leader

The end result of being an outstanding project leader is that you will have the opportunity to be promoted to senior level management jobs within your organization, including director, vice-president, chief operating officer (COO), and others. If you aspire to these roles, it would be a good idea to get an MBA or business degree. You need to think about your career at the beginning to position yourself and gain the necessary experience.

The entry path to project management is wide ranging, but organizations today require project managers to either have completed a project management degree from a university or a certificate program, demonstrating they have the necessary skills for the job.

A second path to project management is on-the-job training. You already work for your organization in another capacity, such as a business analyst, in human resources, organizational change, etc., so they may ask you to lead a project. If your organization has a project management office, you are fortunate, as the office will help you through the learning process and provide necessary tools and training.

If your organization does not have a project management office, you will be responsible for identifying your approach to learning project management practices. In this situation, it is recommended that you pursue the appropriate certification in your country. In the United States the PMP (project management professional) or PgMP (or program management professional, which recognizes advanced experience, skills, and performance in the oversight of multiple related projects) are the standard, while in Europe and Canada, PRINCE2 is the standard.

You will develop the necessary skill set of leadership, technical project management, organization, and business knowledge through on-the-job experience, the best and most common way to learn project management. Numerous studies have shown that 90 percent of our skills and knowledge come from on-the-job experiences. You will need the foundational learning of either a degree or certification to move forward in your career. Take charge of your learning as your organization is always changing. There are significant leaps in technology, the world market is changing, and in general, project management changes so much each year that the way projects were managed five years ago is different from how they are managed today.

However, basic foundational principles, which are detailed in this book, can still be followed.

General Guidelines on Developing Your Leadership

You need to ask yourself what you want to accomplish and what you love doing. Do you want to move into upper management, work in an area you feel passionate about, or find a balance between your personal and professional lives? We need to be decision makers.

The starting point is identifying what you want in your career and what you need to achieve your goal. Choose what you enjoy doing and feel passionate about, if possible. If you are working in a field you absolutely love and are good in, you will be much more successful. If you don't know early in your career, you can try different careers or consult a career planning coach. Once you have identified what you want to do in your career, plan how you can accomplish it. Ask for opportunities and promotions that support it. Make sure you have the necessary training and experience to step into those positions when they become available. Always let your supervisor know what you are interested in pursuing and what you can accomplish for the leaders. Your supervisor cannot read your mind.

As your career progresses, there is increased synergy toward your goals. Enjoy the journey toward your goals, as the path is often not a straight line. Detours will benefit you as you work toward your vision. For example, in college Lisa pursued a teaching career. She selected that career because she loved explaining things to others. Once she began teaching when she graduated at twenty-two, she was exhausted at the end of every day. She realized she did not like standing in front of a classroom, found it challenging to manage the behavior of the students, and realized she did not want to be a teacher. Lisa consulted a career counselor and spend the next three months determining what she really wanted to do based on her natural interests and skills. She selected project management because she was excellent at organization, getting people to work together, and was creative, innovative, and good at technology. She was hired almost immediately as a project leader and loves it. She finds it energizing and exciting. Twenty years later she has moved into a director position and is highly respected by her colleagues and staff. She continues to find her work enjoyable and rewarding each day.

As you work toward your goals, you will experience many challenges. These challenges are events that will help clarify your thoughts and steer you in the right direction. Never consider them failures but new opportunities to learn. Also, don't become overly concerned with criticism. Try to learn from it. Focus on your strengths, what you are doing well, and how you can become better in any area of criticism. Spend your energy working on what you want to accomplish. You are making the world a better place when you work toward your goals by bringing value to the world. Your career will progress steadily if you continue to build skills and bring value to your organization. Another option is to choose to build your career by accepting opportunities from other organizations, possibly the best way to increase your earnings.

Celebrate the small wins because they often bring long-term success. Focus on your mind-set, increase your skill set, always be open to learning, and become the best you can become. By ongoing development and building on your successes, you will have the foundation to sustain your success. Life is an evolution. What we do every day is more important than what we do once a year. It is the small, daily innovations and improvements that lead us to become world class. What we do each day sets us up for the habit of improvement that leads to stunning results.

My mind-set was a major reason for project success. Every day of the project I would think, *Thank you, thank you, thank you for this wonderful project. I love when the team is creative and productive and works well together to deliver the vision and benefits.*

For these projects, the team was always energized, resulting in success for everyone. This mind-set of gratitude produced amazing results. I conducted experiments over the years to verify the impact. On a few projects I told myself I didn't like the project, found the team difficult, or just wanted it to be over. Not surprisingly, these projects tended to be problematic and exhausting.

Prosperity is a reflection of the value you deliver. Focus on how you can be of service to as many people as possible, solve problems and help others be successful. Delivering significant value in life will help you become prosperous and achieve abundance, wealth, and experience joy.

New and better technologies are being introduced into the marketplace. Take advantage of leadership opportunities and training that are offered in your organization or offered to you specifically. This gives you the ability to continually develop more comprehensive leadership skills throughout your career. If you are an independent consultant, a life-changing program can be found at C-Fame Academy at http://bit.ly/cfame-special. This link will give you a discount.

Let's begin by looking at how to build leadership skills when the project is assigned to you.

Building a Foundation for Success (Project Initiation)

YOU HAVE JUST been assigned the project. Where should you start, and what steps should you follow to set it up for success?

In this chapter I give you tools to help you build a foundation for success, to establish yourself as the project leader with the sponsor, stakeholders, and your team, along with guidelines to help you become an amazing communicator. Good communication accounts for 80 percent of project success. All the information covered in this chapter can be used with any project methodology your organization is using as it focuses on leadership, communication, team building, and risk management, which are part of any methodology.

During project initiation, you'll focus primarily on establishing your leadership with the sponsor and stakeholders. The four steps provide detailed information, tools, and resources to help you establish yourself as the leader. Do not become distracted by the overwhelming amount of information you will receive at the start of the project. Instead, focus on these four steps to help your sponsor, stakeholders, and team understand your vision of the project.

Let's briefly look at each step. In step 1 you immediately partner with your sponsor by working one-on-one to identify the high-level scope of the project by developing a project charter together. By involving your sponsor, you close the gap between what the sponsor expects and what the team delivers, thereby increasing project success by 30 percent or more.

In step 2 you establish your leadership ability by presenting the partnership presentation to your sponsor. You seek input from the stakeholders as you develop the first draft of the project scope and identify the risk mitigation process.

These steps help you accomplish three things:

1. the sponsor and your team work to achieve the business goals of the project;
2. you are building high customer satisfaction because you are solving the customer's problem (good risk mitigation solves customers problems and increase their satisfaction by more than 50 percent); and
3. high leader satisfaction is reached with the achievement of the business goals.

In step 3 you identify the project size, which is essential to appropriate planning. Proper planning results in savings of time and money.

In step 4 you prepare for the kickoff and planning session by creating the agenda and planning presentation that allows you to lead the team to success.

Underlying project initiation is the use of project technology to plan and manage your project. New technological resources are changing the project management landscape in amazing and positive ways. By maximizing the use of technology, you can focus on value-added activities such as communication, problem resolution, and leading the team rather than tactical activities. To be seen as a leader, you need to interact with the sponsor, stakeholders, and team members.

Following are long-term benefits of building a foundation for success:

- High sponsor and stakeholders satisfaction gets you noticed for new opportunities;

- Create an award-winning productive team, ensuring positive project results;
- Complete projects faster and on budget; and
- Resolve risks before the problems occur by following an innovative process.

Let's now begin the initiate phase of building a foundation for success. The graph below summarizes the four steps of building a foundation for success. Across from each step are the required deliverables and the optional resources. These are designed to establish you as the leader of the project and to deliver the project successfully.

BUILDING A FOUNDATION FOR SUCCESS
(Project Initiation)

Step	Required Deliverables	Optional Deliverables
Step 1: Project Manager Is Assigned Project	• Project Creation Form • Placeholder created in Project Tracking Tool	• Checklist: Project Initiation
Step 2: Obtain Sponsor / Stakeholder Input	• Project Process • Project Scope • Risk Register • Risk Worksheet	• Sponsor/Stakeholder Interview Form • PM Self-Assessment
Step 3: Project Sizing Tool	• Project Sizing Tool	• Project Sizing Tool Directions
Step 4: Prepare for Planning Session	• Agenda – Planning Session • Presentation	• Importance of Project Planning • Checklist: Project Initiation

Each step has a separate section describing what you need to do. The remainder of this chapter will discuss each step in-detail. It might be helpful to refer back to this graphic as you read the chapter. We begin with step 1: the project manager is assigned a project.

At the beginning of each chapter I will showcase David, who is one of the most impressive project leaders I know. Here is his story.

David's Story: Building a Foundation

David is thirty, successful, and looking forward to a promising future in his company. After graduation he found a job in project management, getting a good entry-level job for a major firm. His life is unfolding according to plan. He has a degree in project management and is certified as a project management professional (PMP certification). He would like to work in project management for another year or two and then move into a leadership position.

Two years ago, wanting more opportunities, he accepted a position at his current company, a large manufacturing organization.

"I make very good money, and I get promoted on the fast track," David says. "The price is total dedication, and like many in my company. I spend a minimum of fifty hours at work every week. Frankly, I enjoy this. This is me."

David is quite good at his job. He is always open to new challenges, learning new skills, making new contacts, and attending webinars and classes to stay current in his profession. His career is moving ahead, and he has been getting steady promotions.

Now that he's thirty, he pays closer attention to exercise—he jogs regularly and watches his weight, two things that hadn't really been part of his lifestyle in his twenties. He is married to Marla, whom he describes as smart and funny and beautiful; she works in the financial sector. They have a one-year-old son.

David says, "We make a great team."

When he came to work last week, his manager called him into his office to ask him to handle a high-profile project, an international project involving end-of-lease contracts for servers. (The company leases more than a thousand servers for more than ten different applications.)

The initial contracts are reviewed by business leaders and signed off by the legal department. The challenge the company is facing is that the renewal dates are often missed, resulting in millions of dollars in fines. When contracts become past due, the vendors stop providing support, which impacts not only company revenue but that of customers using the servers. The company is constantly updating their technology to use cutting-edge technology and misses due dates because new technology overlaps the old technology for a few months. Each application is handled by eight different departments responsible for different processes, and there is a lack of positive communication between the departments, with frequent blaming occurring.

The sponsor, Ted, based in Europe, is highly demanding and quick to criticize. The stakeholders are based in Europe, Asia, and the United States. The overall purpose of the project is to develop a process to reduce the number of missed renewal dates and to identify the root cause of the communication difficulties among the departments. His manager tells him he was selected to lead the project because of his skills in processing and problem solving. Because of the different time zones involved, he will need to either work early or late to accommodate the needs of the team. David has never worked with the sponsor before but has worked successfully on other projects with many of the stakeholders. David will not need to travel and can work with his team through electronic face-to-face meetings. David agreed to take the project, and his manager communicated to the sponsor and stakeholders that he would be handling the project.

The next day David sent an email to Ted, the project sponsor, introducing himself and scheduling a half hour meeting to discuss the one-page project charter. The next day Ted and David met face-to-face via an electronic meeting to discuss the charter. Ted was appreciative that David reached out to him on his vision for the project. David finalized the project charter and sent it to Ted. David also accessed the electronic tracking tool and created the project by entering the title, sponsor, stakeholders, and himself as the project manager. To prepare himself for the next steps, he reviewed the checklist for project initiation.

David was extremely busy during the next few weeks, setting up the foundation for the project. During the initial meeting to discuss the charter, David had told Ted he would be scheduling a half hour meeting to review the methodology.

David spends three hours preparing the presentation. He includes the work that is completed during project initiation, planning, execution, monitoring, control, and project close. He includes information on sponsor responsibilities, team responsibilities, project manager responsibilities, quality reviews of the project, and project update frequency with Ted. He then spends an hour practicing the presentation until he can complete it easily within half an hour.

During the meeting, Ted is actively involved and asks many questions. He listens carefully as David explained the sponsor's (Ted's) responsibilities and added a few more ways he could help make the project a success. It was an extremely positive meeting, and Ted expressed his confidence in having David manage the project. It was the first time a project manager had made this type of presentation to Ted, and it significantly increased his confidence in a successful outcome. At the end of the meeting, David and Ted discussed the process to select project team members. David would contact the managers and supervisors in the fifteen departments in order to identify team members.

After the meeting, David sent an email to the managers and supervisors regarding team selection and asked for their recommendations. They identified team members and their role on the project, and David then sent an email to each team member selected. David, the managers, and the supervisor then sent a joint email notifying each team member they had been selected, their role in the project, and that they would receive additional information in the next few days. David then sent an invitation to each team member and Ted to attend the kickoff and planning meeting. He asked Ted to attend for the first fifteen minutes to discuss the importance of the project to the team and to answer any questions.

Next, in preparation for completing the detailed scope, Ted arranged short half hour meetings with the four stakeholders individually, allowing him to focus on their answers and expectations. He used the sponsor/stakeholder interview form to ensure consistency. Using the information he gathered, David then developed the detailed scope and began identifying risks and the mitigation process.

Part of planning a project appropriately is understanding its impact on the organization. David completed the project sizing tool and determined it was a midsized project based on the criteria of his organization. He was now ready to develop the agenda and then the kickoff and planning presentation to be used during that meeting. It took him about two hours to complete the agenda and presentation because he kept adding graphics and streamlining it. He is now ready to facilitate the meeting.

To summarize, David has established himself as a strong leader with Ted, his sponsor, and has created a foundation for the success of his project through his partnership with the sponsor and stakeholders. He has clearly communicated with the team members on their roles in the project.

Step 1: Project Leader Is Assigned Project

Required deliverables for step 1 are

- project charter
- placeholder created in tracking tool

The optional deliverable is

- checklist: project initiation

Your organization has decided to move forward with the project and you have been assigned the project manager. It is best to establish yourself as the project leader immediately because your actions are the critical success factors. All the tools and processes are designed to help you further develop your leadership skills. Project Initiation, the process of creating a foundation for success, is time intensive and requires a significant amount of work. If this work is skipped or ignored, it is almost impossible to bring the project to a successful conclusion and or go back and make revisions. Although these steps may appear elementary, the actual skills demonstrating leadership, communication, creating high performing teams and utilizing technology appropriately can expedite a career. Do not underestimate the importance of demonstrating these skills from the beginning of the project. It may be impossible to be seen as a leader if you have not demonstrated these qualities from the beginning.

Before we begin, congratulate yourself on accepting the assignment. Being a project leader requires you to have a wide range of skills and good judgement to determine how to manage the project effectively, consider the complexity and scope of the project, the best methodology to use and how to customize it to the project and the culture of the organization to support project management practices. And if that is not challenging enough, the project management landscape is always changing and you need to find time to stay current with the changes. Becoming a successful project leader prepares you for future roles.

Let's begin by looking at the required deliverables and how and why you use them to clearly identify yourself as the project leader. As the project leader you are responsible for planning and delivering business results. A project sponsor has been assigned with overall accountability for the project to ensure the project delivers the agreed business benefits. Only by partnering with the sponsor can you provide the leadership needed to deliver the agreed business benefits.

Your partnership with the sponsor begins with the project charter, a one-page description of the project that you and the sponsor create together, giving you both a better understanding of the agreed business benefits.

The form is used to

- formally recognize the project;
- describe the project (in one page).

It is completed jointly by the sponsor and project manager and is divided into six sections, including

1. Business case (two to three sentence description);
2. Opportunity statement (identify the opportunity, what needs to be changed or improved, etc.);
3. Goal statement (state the overall goal and then the steps to complete the goal);

4. Project scope in summary form (identify what is in and out of the scope of the project);

5. Estimated project plan (identify milestones and target dates); and

6. Team members (list sponsor, stakeholders, project manager, subject matter experts, etc.).

The project charter is usually completed within the first week after you are assigned the project. Below is an example of a project charter. You can adjust this form to the needs of the organization.

(PROJECT CHARTER) Security Technology Services Re-Organization	
Business Case	**Opportunity Statement**
This project will execute and validate the processes required to complete the addition and alignment of a Vice President from division 430 to division 269 as part of the re-organization effort.	• Executing the Technology Services Reorganization Project will provide: • Clear direction and focus for the team to know when, who, and how to complete necessary changes • All changes driven from the reorg is recorded and validated in timely manner • Increased productivity requiring minimal re-work • Accurate reporting • Ensure appropriate transfer of people, capital assets, expenses and recoveries
Goal Statement	**Project Scope**
Y: Move and verify personnel, capital assets, expenses and recoveries associated with the Business System Transformation Re-organization. X_1: Validation of Organizational Reporting, Charging and Recoveries. X_2: Reduced time it takes to complete organizational changes. X_3: Coordinated effort across and within impacted Departments X_4: Validation of PMO Reorganization Process. X_5: Multiple system updates are required whenever personnel and or program changes occur.	**In-Scope:** Organizational moves associated with Technology Systems Transformation Impacted systems: PeopleSoft, CLUES, IO Navigator, Primavera, General Ledger, Business Statement Tool, PSRs and related processes, and other Procurement systems, Capital Management System, CPS Metrics **Out-of-Scope:** Interim Assignments, and Departments not impacted
Estimated Project Plan	**Team Members**
Milestone — Target Teams reviews Scope — 27-April-2019 Project planning session — 28-April 2019 Project Completion — 30-June-2019	Sponsor: Karen Thomas Stakeholders: John Enders, Kite Klein, Jeff Tipper Program Manager: Susan Niles Project Manager: Joy Tom Plan Analyst: TBD Team Members: Meryl Nam, Moyer Tern, Zu Won

After you and the sponsor have completed the one-page, high-level project charter, you then have some basic information to begin drafting the detailed scope document, which is discussed in chapter 2, project planning.

The other required deliverable in step 1 is to create a placeholder for your project in the project management software tool your organization is using. First let's talk briefly about the benefits of using an electronic project tracking tool.

Enhanced technology improves project management by

- *Utilizing data storage and backup:* It is now possible to store data on cloud computing or on secure drives, thus allowing the team to access and share files as needed, ensuring that your project will not fail because of data loss.
- *Online collaboration and communication:* Instant communication can include instant messaging, email, telephone, video call, WebEx, Skype, Twitter, Facebook, and more. Project teams can work in any location and still be connected.
- *Managing deadlines:* With new software, the team can stay on schedule and complete tasks per the project plan. The team is aware of the deadlines and the connections between all the tasks that need to be completed and in what sequence.
- *Creating a project budget:* There are many excellent project management software programs that have simplified managing the budget because it is built into the program.
- *Spending time on tasks:* New project management software is available that help you track the time spent on each task and the project.
- *Creating a project snapshot:* New project software provides fast and accurate project information to the team and sponsors. Many also allow a view of the progress from start to finish.

Project tracking tools help increase project efficiency, allowing the project leader to focus on the value add and important components of leading the team and communication. This creates a winning project. It is impossible to manage projects effectively without software.

Parts of the placeholder include the project name, expected start and end dates (which almost always change), project manager, sponsor, and a brief description of the project using the project charter, and any other information required by your organization. After you have created a placeholder for your project, the software will need to be populated with resources, tasks, timelines, etc. after the project plan has been created during the planning meeting. You have now completed the two required deliverables: the project charter and have created *a* placeholder in the project management software.

Next, let's look at the optional deliverable, which is the checklist for project initiation. The checklist is a summary of all required activities to be completed during project initiation. It is good to review it at the end of step 1 to verify that the two required deliverables have been completed. It also helps you identify all remaining required deliverables for project initiation and helps you plan your work.

Below is a representative listing of activities to include in the checklist for project initiation. The sample checklist shows that the first two deliverables we discussed in step 1 were completed. The remaining deliverables will be completed during steps 2–4. Each organization creates a customized checklist based on their methodology and culture. If your organization has not developed a checklist, it would be a good opportunity for you to demonstrate leadership and create one.

Sample Checklist: Building a Foundation for Success (Project Initiation)

Completed	Step	Activity
Yes	1	Completed project charter with input from sponsor and key stakeholders
	1	Created placeholder in project management software
No	2	Created partnership presentation and presented to sponsor
No	2	Created draft of scope (secured sponsor input/ approval)

No	2	Analyzed project impacts (risk register and worksheet)
No	3	Identified project size
No	4	Prepared for and scheduled planning meeting
No	4	Prepared kickoff and planning presentation

Step 2: Obtain Sponsor/Stakeholder Input

The required deliverables for step 2 are

- Project process (project partnership presentation)
- Project scope (detailed document)
- Risk worksheet
- Risk register

The optional deliverables are

- Sponsor/stakeholder interview form
- Project manager self-assessment

You are now ready to move to step 2. It is during this step that you clearly become a leader of the project, and it begins with the project partnership presentation. After I met with the sponsor to complete the project charter, I would then schedule a second half-hour meeting to discuss the partnership presentation. This presentation and discussion were one of the main reasons for my success, and I will now share it so you can also benefit from it.

The project partnership presentation is a short, half-hour discussion with the sponsor that covers the process and methodology, what to expect at each phase of the project, and success factors and expectations. At the end of the discussion, the sponsor will have a clear vision of how you will manage the project, expectations, and how to assist to ensure success. Below, I've included the points that will be discussed during this meeting, summarized by topics and bullet points that are intuitive and easy to follow and present. The more you can openly discuss these points with the sponsor, the more successful your project. It is helpful to spend a good amount of time preparing for the discussion so you can present it factually and easily. Practice before presenting to your sponsor. You want to emphasize your leader skills and come across as confident and in control.

You can use the information below to prepare your presentation. Each heading is a separate slide. It is a good idea to add graphics to a professional presentation.

Project Partnership Presentation

Agenda

- Project manager success factors
- Project requirements
- Project phases
- Sponsor success factors
- Project manager responsibilities to sponsor
- Quality review checklist
- Team member expectations
- Project update meetings with sponsor

Project Manager Success Factors

- High-value tasks
  - Sponsor/stakeholder partnership
  - Risk management
  - Team performance focus

You will want to emphasize that you will be focused on forming a strong partnership with the sponsor and stakeholder, solving risks and problems, and developing high-performing teams. Emphasize that you will be focused on communicating with the team. The combination of these factors will help increase project success by more than 70 percent.

Project Requirements

- Scope management
  - Description of activities and deliverables included in the project. Provides the standard for evaluating requested changes are to be included.
- Risk management
  - Can identify and assess business risks for tracking/ reporting and proactive mitigation.
- Schedule management
  - Project schedule (project work plan).
- Project reviews
  - Ensure sponsor, key stakeholder, and customer are on the same page prior to moving to the next phase.
- Project status reports
  - Organizes and summarizes the project information and presents the results of any analysis.
- Resource management
  - The correct budgeting of resources based on task requirements.

These basic project requirements are fairly standard for all projects.

Project Phases

Discuss what occurs during project initiation, planning, execution, monitoring, control, project close, the required and optional deliverables, and expected outcome. A chapter is devoted to each phase.

- Building a foundation for success (project initiation)
- Creating amazing teams (project planning)
- Delivering project success (execute, monitor, control)
- Accelerating your career (project close)

Sponsor Success Factors

This discussion clarifies the importance of the sponsor's involvement in the success of the project.

Sponsor Responsibilities

- Partners with project manager to prepare draft of scope
- Attends first fifteen minutes of kickoff/planning meeting
- Removes project barriers
- Identifies frequency of update meeting with project manager
- Identifies required project reports and frequency
- Identifies additional requirements of the project
- Participates in project reviews (reviews and signs off on presentation prior to meeting with stakeholders)

This is very important to cover. The sponsor knows what is expected of her or him, thus facilitating a much smoother project overall. All projects encounter challenges and barriers, and you will need the sponsor's support at times to remove them.

Project Manager's Responsibilities to Sponsor

- Conducts scheduled meetings/updates
- Provides weekly project updates
- Provides project reports based on sponsor requests
- Prepares and reviews all presentations with sponsor prior to presentation
- Stores project team documentation in one centralized location accessible to all involved parties

This discussion helps the sponsor understand how you will interact with him or her on the project.

Quality Checklist Review

- The project manager reviews the quality review checklist, which is a summary of what the project manager will complete during the project and keep leadership updated. This list is identified by the organization and includes the following:
  - Manage scope
  - Identify team expectations
  - Create project plan
  - Manage project plan in software tool
  - Manage communication plan

This discussion helps the sponsor understand how the quality review will be conducted.

Team Member Expectations

- The project manager reviews the team member expectations and adjusts based on sponsor requests. Team member expectations:
  - Completes tasks based on project plan and updates in the project tracking tool per the schedule;
  - Attends status meetings. If unable to attend, notifies project manager;
  - Completes all activities based on schedule or notifies project manager if unable to complete;
  - Keeps calendar up-to-date;
  - Notifies project manager of risks/issues as they arise;
  - Reads and responds to team communication in a timely manner; and
  - Treats all team members with respect—listens, and asks clarifying questions

This discussion allows the sponsor to add any additional expectations if needed.

Project Update Meetings with Sponsor

- The project manager asks the sponsor to identify the frequency and type of communication the sponsor requires, such as weekly via one-on-one meetings, database updates, etc. This ensures clear communication and provides the type of project information the sponsor needs.

Congratulations! You have now discussed the project partnership with your sponsor. If your sponsor requests follow-up, complete any follow up items from the meeting.

Scope Document

You are now ready to develop the first draft of the scope document using information from the project charter. As the project leader, you develop the first draft of the scope, a lengthy document that takes time to complete appropriately.

In the next chapter, I discuss how the draft is reviewed and revised by the project team members during the kickoff and planning meeting. The final scope document is then shared with the sponsor, and any additional revisions are made based on the sponsor's feedback.

The project scope document

- Provides a complete picture of the project and details the purpose, benefits, objectives, success indicators, budget, and committed key dates for a project;
- Defines the work required to successfully complete the project and provides a common understanding of the goal;
- Is completed jointly by the sponsor and project manager and then reviewed and revised by the project team; and
- Is a living document that is updated throughout the project.

Outline for a Scope Document

Project Name

Purpose

A short paragraph that defines the purpose of this project as identified on the project charter.

Benefits

The benefits of doing this project—why we are doing this project.

Objectives

This lists the targeted accomplishments for this project: what the team will be held accountable for. Objectives should be specific, measurable, and attainable. These are action items.

Project Scope

Defines the boundaries and limits of the project. Document if this project is part of a program.

In-scope: Lists any details that will help to further define the boundaries of the project.

Out-of-scope: List any items that will be specifically excluded from the scope of this project.

Deliverables

The tangible things that this project will produce/deliver to complete the project and that the customer is "willing to pay for."

Project Budget

What has the program manager budgeted for this project? This should be refined once the project schedule has been finalized and resources loaded.

Project Success Indicators

How high is the bar being set (target date, quality objectives, etc.)? How will this project be judged as successful when it is finished?

User/Business Unit Impact

Describe which business units are impacted, how and when they are impacted, and what involvement they should have in this change.

External Dependencies

Is this project dependent upon completion of deliverables from other projects/initiatives? Are other projects dependent on this project?

Key Project Dates

Identify any key dates that this project will be expected to meet, include driving dates (those that must be met due to regulatory or other business reasons).

Change Threshold

Define date/cost/quality change thresholds under which the project manager can make change decisions, over which the sponsor and/or key stakeholders must decide.

Team Organizations

Project sponsor
Key stakeholders
Process owner
Project manager

Team Members names, project roles, resource allocation percentage (the amount of time each resource is approved to work on this project; it should be provided by the sponsor)

Constraints

This section lists all the limitations facing this project that cannot be changed. Note whether one constraint takes precedence over the others (e.g., if the target date is imposed by federal regulation, then it may be the primary constraint and take on more importance than a cost constraint).

Risks

High-impact or high-likelihood events that could negatively impact this project but may be dealt with by project activities to avoid, mitigate, and/or manage the risk. Risks may be related to costs, technology, operations, organizations, resources, etc.

Assumptions

List the items that this project relies on that are expected to occur (any delay in the requirements of this project will directly impact the final production schedule).

Definitions (as used in the project)

Include all necessary definitions to ensure a common understanding of the team.

You have now completed the draft of scope document. We will next look at the risk worksheet.

Risk Worksheet

The risk worksheet and register work together. The risk worksheet is a simple document used to identify risks and the process for resolution and can be used as is or used to populate the risk register.

The risk worksheet contains columns for

- Negative risks/risk opportunities
- Probability that it will occur
- Impact
- Risk score
- Responses where additional information can be added to help manage and resolve the risk

Risk Register

The risk register is a comprehensive document that helps you identify, analyze, and mitigate risks for the project. It contains four main categories:

1. Risk identification
   - Determines which risks might affect the project and documents their characteristics
   - Provides a description of and ranks the risk for impact on the project
2. Quantification
   - Significance of the risk
   - Rank
3. Control
   - Appropriate action type for each risk
     - Accept = accept the risk and do nothing at this time
     - Mitigate = take action to minimize risk
     - Contingent = take action only if risk materializes
     - Transfer = shift risk to another organization/individual
   - Identify the owner of the risk
   - Set a target date for the action to be completed
4. Implementation
   - Maintain an action log

- Date implemented
- Current status

The risk register is a living document and is updated throughout the life of the project. The project manager should review it with the sponsor frequently during the life of the project. At times the sponsor will need to step in and help resolve the risks. At a minimum, the sponsor should always be informed of all risks and the planned mitigation.

Below is a sample risk register created in Excel. You can also include tabs along the bottom for Instructions on how to complete the risk register and another tab for risk examples. This type of risk register is useful as you can easily evaluate potential risks by reviewing the risk examples.

RISK REGISTER									
Risk Identification		Quantification		Control			Implementation		
ID	Description	Significance (10 high, 1 Low)	Rank	Action	Owner	Date	Action Log	Date	Status

Risk Register | Instructions | Risk Examples

It is helpful to create a general risk categories document that you can use as a starting point for all your projects to identify potential risks. Below is a listing of twelve risk categories. As new risks occur in your projects, add them in the appropriate category.

Below are some categories of risks, a good starting point.

Risk Categories

- Resources
- Funding
- Scope
- Change management

- Planning
- Technology
- Project management
- Development process
- Corporate environment
- Integration
- Testing
- Quality

I've included a few examples of risks below. Correctly identifying risks and mitigating them in your project will significantly increase the success of your project.

Potential Project Risks

Resources
    ✓ Resource requirements not estimated—resource usage not managed
    ✓ Not enough resources to meet desired target date
    ✓ Resource availability not as high as planned in schedule
Funding
    ✓ Project funding is not committed or secure
    ✓ No historic information available for project estimates
    ✓ Project is not funded at the appropriate level
Scope
    ✓ Scope has not been clearly defined before work started
    ✓ Deliverables have not been clearly defined
    ✓ Scope not approved by stakeholders

You have now completed the four required deliverables for step 2:

- Project process (project partnership presentation)
- Project scope (detailed document)
- Risk worksheet
- Risk register

We are now ready to discuss the optional deliverables. They include

- Sponsor/stakeholder interview form
- Project manager self-assessment

The sponsor/stakeholder interview form contains an extensive list of questions to ask the sponsor and stakeholder that you will need in order to complete the scope document and before the planning session can begin. I've included a few questions that can be included below. One way to develop the form is to use the scope document to prepare the questions. Interview sponsor and selected stakeholders individually. Your organization may have a similar document in place.

Sample Sponsor/Stakeholder Interview Form

1. Project background (what caused this project to happen? Describe project purpose).
2. Which program is this project associated with?
3. Describe the objectives of this project (What goals need to be met for the project to be successful?).
4. What are the benefits from this project (cost reduction, better utilization of resources, increase customer satisfaction, improved system uptime, etc.)?
5. Does this project have sustainable development impact/benefits for the environment, for economic/governance, and/or social benefits?
6. What are the performance goals?
7. Are there product financial targets?
8. What are project cost targets or budget? Has funding been approved?
9. Are there Sarbanes-Oxley, regulatory, or ergonomic implications or issues?
10. Scope: A. Describe the project scope; B. What is in scope? C. What is out of scope?
11. Should this project be broken into multiple projects?

12. What are the key deliverables?
13. What are the key desired dates? What is driving these dates?
14. How is this project prioritized in relation to other projects?
15. Who are the team members, their functions, and their availability?
16. Are there any limitations or constraints?
17. Are there known risks?
18. Define successful project completion.
19. How often do you want to receive status updates? In what format? What information?
20. What is the escalation process for issues and change requests?

The project manager self-assessment form is for your private use as the project manager to review the project to help you develop a complete understanding of the project. You can use it as a prep document to make sure you can explain the project to the sponsor and stakeholders before my conversations with them. At a high level, can you explain the methodology you are using for the project, describe the scope, risks and risk mitigation plan, resource management, gate review schedule, communication plan, and technology.

Sample Project Manager Self-Assessment Form

1. Who is the project sponsor?
2. Is this project aligned to a program?
3. If aligned, who is the program manager?
4. Who are the key stakeholders?
5. What project management methodology will be used?
6. What are the project deliverables? What does the project sponsor expect the team to produce?
7. Who is on the project team?
8. Do the team members have expertise in the subject areas needed for the project?
9. How will the team members report their time on this project on their timesheets?

10. What is the project start date?
11. Is there a desired completion date? What is the driver?
12. What are the issues (concerns/assumptions/constraints) in completing the project?
13. What is the business benefit of doing this project?
14. What tool will be used to maintain the project schedule (Microsoft Project, Primavera, or other tools)?
15. Is my team familiar with using project management processes? Do I need to train the team?

Step 3: Identify Project Sizing

The required deliverable for step 3 is

- Project sizing tool

The optional deliverable is

- Directions on use of tool

You are ready to move to step 3 to identify project sizing. Now that you have received sponsor/stakeholder input and have an understanding of the project scope, you are ready to complete the project sizing tool. If you have all required information to fill out the form, this is a fairly quick step to complete but important to the success of the project. The project sizing tool helps you identify the impact of the project on the organization.

This tool helps you identify whether the size of your project is small, medium, or large; the impact on the organization; and the required resources.

- A small project may involve only one supervisor and manager and their staff while a large project would impact multiple areas and departments in the organization.

- The size of your project will help you identify which deliverables you will need to complete.
- The tool I have included is fairly intuitive and walks you through the process.

By definition, a large project impacts the organization more broadly than small projects. Each organization has their own definition to include on the project sizing tool. I included generic definitions and you will need to adjust them based on the needs of your organization.

The example below evaluates the impact of the project on the organization by looking at seven characteristics and ratings of each by using points of 9, 3, or 1. The final number determines the project impact on the organization and the project size. This tool will need to be adjusted based on the needs of the organization.

Create a table with five columns labeled: Impact, 9 points, 3 points, and 1 point for this project. The seven generic characteristics below are listed under impact. Total points for all seven characteristics determine the size of the project.

The Seven Generic Characteristics:

- Project Complexity
  - ✓ (9 points) Highly complex, large team, many stakeholders
  - ✓ (3 points) Medium complexity, smaller scope, narrower focus, fewer stakeholders
  - ✓ (1 point) Low complexity, limited scope, small team, short duration
- Project Risk
  - ✓ (9 points) High significance
  - ✓ (3 points) Medium significance
  - ✓ (1 Point) Low significance
- Areas that need to assign resources to the project
  - ✓ (9 points) Greater than 6 areas
  - ✓ (3 points) 4–6 areas
  - ✓ (1 point) 3 areas or fewer

- Number of departments impacted by the project
  - ✓ (9 points) Greater than 6 areas
  - ✓ (3 points) 4–6 areas
  - ✓ (1 point) 3 areas or fewer
- Estimated Cost
  - ✓ (9 points) $1M or greater
  - ✓ (3 points) Less than $1M and greater than $50K
  - ✓ (1 point) Less than $50K
- New Technology
  - ✓ (9 points) Unproven, new technology
  - ✓ (3 points) Proven technology, but not deployed in company
  - ✓ (1 point) Proven technology, and deployed in company
- Number of people impacted if project is not successful
  - ✓ (9 points) Greater than 800
  - ✓ (3 points) 201–800
  - ✓ (1 point) 1–200

In the example above, a large impact project scores at above 50, a medium impact project scores between 27 and 50, and a small impact project scores fewer than 27.

Step 4: Prepare for Planning Session

The required deliverables for step 4 are
- Agenda for kickoff and planning meeting
- Planning session presentation

The optional deliverables are
- Importance of project planning
- Checklist: project initiation

You are now ready to complete step 4, preparing for the planning session. Knowing the impact of the project on the organization helps you plan appropriately. Team members are identified in partnership with your sponsor, managers, and supervisors. All team members are notified by a joint email from you and their supervisor that they will be part of the team and the role they will play. You then schedule the kickoff and planning meeting. The project kickoff meeting sets the stage for your project. If you nail the kickoff, your team starts the project focused, energized, and motivated. Good kickoff meetings don't just happen. They take planning and preparation.

Next, you prepare the agenda for the kickoff and planning meeting. The agenda contains the steps that need to be completed during the planning session. Keep the kickoff meeting short and simple, usually less than half an hour. This is the time for you to establish leadership and earn the confidence of your team. The kickoff meeting includes introductions by the team and their role in the project (you and their supervisor have already notified them of the participation and role in the project prior to the meeting), sponsor discussion on the project importance with questions and answers, a review of the project methodology that will be followed and clarifying team expectations.

The planning meeting immediately follows the kickoff meeting and has two main agenda items, the review of the scope and developing the project plan. It is essential that the team is involved in reviewing and revising the scope document, including what's required for the project to be successful. Additionally, the team is involved in identifying the deliverables, activities, activity owners, and activity duration. The project will usually fail if the team is not involved in those two agenda items. Team feedback and participation in planning the project and decision making helps you strengthen your leadership and build a high performing, motivated team.

Below is a sample project planning agenda that lists the topics that need to be discussed. The agenda should be customized for each project and adjusted based on the needs of the organization.

Sample Kickoff and Project Planning Agenda

- Introductions: facilitator, project sponsor, key project/ stakeholders, project manager, team members;
- Conduct project sponsor kickoff with question and answer session;

- Review project management process/methodology that will be used;
- Identify team expectations;
- Review and refine project scope document;
- Develop project activity network (sticky note exercise);
- Identify activity owners and estimate activity durations;
- Identify key milestones;
- Enter project activity network into project management tool;
- Schedule project and perform schedule compression and determine risk response duration;
- Generate and distribute activity identification sheet forms;
- Review/revise the project management plan; and
- Assess project risk and develop risk response activities.

After you have identified the topics, you then need to build a presentation covering each of the topics in the agenda. The purpose of the project kickoff and planning presentation is to guide the team members through the planning meeting and begin creating a high-performing team. The meeting may be only an hour for a small project or extend over days for a large, complex project. I have found that preparing for and presenting this presentation at the kickoff and planning meeting helps me create a highly productive team with everyone working together and the team supporting the goals of the project. Of particular importance was covering the team expectations. I will talk more about this in the next chapter.

Below is a sample of topics and content that can be included in the presentation. Take the time to create a quality presentation. It will help establish you as the leader of the team. You can use the sample presentation below with topics and content to develop your presentation. In the next chapter I will discuss how to use this presentation with your team.

Sample Presentation for Kickoff and Planning Meeting Agenda

- Introductions: facilitator, project sponsor, key project/ stakeholders, project manager, team members;
- Conduct project sponsor kickoff with question and answer session;
- Ground rules laid out;
- Identify team expectations;
- Review project management process/methodology that will be used;
- Review and refine project scope document;
- Identify project deliverables;
- Develop project activity network (sticky note exercise); and
- Identify activity owners and estimate activity durations.

Ground Rules for Meetings

- Breaks will occur every 1 to 1.5 hours;
- We will start and resume *on time;*
- One conversation at a time, please;
- Concentrate on what we are doing here, not some other distraction;
- Focus on *what* needs to be done, not *how* to do it; and
- Allow the project manager (person conducting the planning session) to do his or her job without interruption.

Team Expectations for the Project

- Attend status meetings when required (whether in-person or virtual). Attendance is mandatory. If unable to attend, you are expected to update your status before the meeting;
- Update your status weekly via the tool added by the project manager;
- Complete all activities per the schedule that was developed by the team. If you are unable to complete activities per the schedule, immediately notify the project manager;
- Keep calendars updated;

- Identify issues and risks;
- Read all team communication in a timely manner;
- Treat all team members with respect;
- Team to identify escalation process; and
- Project documentation to be stored in a centralized location for easy access.

Team Members

- Sponsor
- Key stakeholders
- Process owner
- Project manager:
- Team members
- Customers and vendors

Planning Session Deliverables

- Finalize scope
- Activities (three-step process)
- Identify activities
- Identify flow of activities on each sheet (on-sheet)
- Identify dependencies across all sheets (off-sheet)
- Identify task owners
- Estimate duration of tasks
- Project ID
- Project name

Identify Project Activities

- Brief description of the activity
- Identify owner (versus resource) of activity
- Owner identifies resource to complete activities
- Owner guides resource to complete activities
- Owner reports status to project manager
- Resource completes the activities

Sample Workflow

- Included in prepared sample with the link.

All Other Important Information

- Customized to project and organization.

You have now completed the required deliverables for step 4, preparing for the planning session:

- Agenda for kickoff and planning meeting
- Planning session presentation

Next let's discuss the optional deliverables. They include

- The importance of project planning
- Project checklist: project initiation

It is important that you are able to articulate the importance of project planning to your sponsors, stakeholders, and team. Appropriate planning is essential to project success. Be able to explain the difference between being a prevent-it organization or a fix-it organization and mitigating risks before they become a mountain of problems. Often, if there is not a strong risk management mitigation plan in place, the problems escalate and can become so overwhelming that often they cannot be resolved. This can be avoided with appropriate planning.

Organizations and project leaders may be eager to get going on their projects. At times, from their perspective, planning is wasted time—time that interferes with and unnecessarily delays progress. Some organization do not have the culture nor the structure to support project planning. In such organization, action is more rewarded than careful planning efforts. However, planning the project appropriately is most important for success and to avoid rework during the execution phase of the project. A direct correlation exists between the quality of a project plan and the quality of the execution of the project. Project planning prevents significant rework. One hour of planning can save from twenty to two hundred hours of corrective action later.

Identifying problems during planning allows the team to mitigate and resolve issues early, and the project can proceed smoothly during the execution phase. Without problem identification and mitigation in the planning phase, issues can grow and basically become unsolvable.

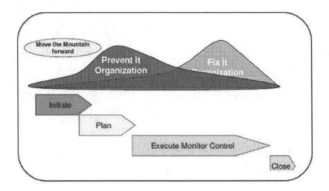

In step 1, the project leader is assigned the project, we looked at the checklist for project initiation. Now that you have completed the four steps of building a foundation for your project, review the checklist again to verify that you have completed all necessary deliverables.

This sample checklist shows that all the items we discussed for steps 1–4 have been completed.

Sample Checklist: Building a Foundation for Success (Project Initiation)

Completed Step Activity

Completed	Step	Activity
Yes	1	Completed project charter with input from sponsor and key stakeholders
Yes	1	Created placeholder in project management software

Yes	2	Created partnership presentation and presented to sponsor
Yes	2	Created draft of scope (secured sponsor input and approval)
Yes	2	Analyzed project impacts (risk register and worksheet)
Yes	3	Identified project size
Yes	4	Prepared for and scheduled planning meeting
Yes	4	Prepared kickoff and planning presentation
Yes	4	Identified all team members and sent invitations to planning meeting

Summary

Great job completing the four steps of project initiation, building a foundation for success that established your leadership role with your sponsor, stakeholders, and team. Two of the required deliverables are presentations that are impactful and important but also time intensive to develop. The benefit of the presentations is that they help you clearly establish yourself as a leader.

In this chaper you built a strong foundation of project success by partnering with your sponsor and stakeholders, created a first draft of the scope, identified the risk mitigation process and the size of the project, and planned the kickoff and planning meeting by preparing a presentation. Wow! Project initiation in project management is a lot of work but pays huge dividends during the remainder of the project. Great job at completing the four steps of building a foundation for success during project initiation.

Congratulation! You are now ready to move to planning the project and can begin to create an amazing team.

Creating Amazing Teams
(Project Planning)

NOW THAT YOU are seen as a leader by your sponsor and stakeholders and have created a foundation of success for your project, you are ready to start building an amazing team.

During project planning, you will focus on establishing your leadership with your team. You do this by building a high-performing team. This is accomplished by involving them in the planning, risk, and project-review process. An important skill you will need is clear, concise communication when creating an amazing team.

The four steps to project planning provide detailed information, tools, and resources. Your team will rely on you to provide guidance as the project is planned. Focus on these four steps to help you create a highly productive team that will help make the project a success and is fun to lead.

In step 1 you conduct the planning meeting. Involving the team in the planning, helping to build the project plan including activities, tasks, owners, resources, timelines, etc. helps to create an involved, committed team. One way to demonstrate your leadership is by promoting and creating success for your team. Teams on successful projects are more confident and significantly more productive.

The planning meeting will be discussed in detail in this chapter, but I would like to emphasize two points. It is important to identify team expectations and have them verbally agree to them. This simple process helps create a strong team. It is also important to have everyone review and revise the draft scope document. Each team member has different expertise that contribute to an accurate and comprehensive scope. Working together to develop the scope helps ensure alignment and agreement to project goals. Working together, overcoming the challenges involved in all projects, encouraging the team to use and expand their skills, and recognizing their contributions helps develop a cohesive, highly productive team.

In step 2 you continue to build a high-performing team by involving them in identifying risks and creating a risk-management process. Working together, they can often resolve risks before they escalate, a major factor in project success. In this step you also develop your communication plan.

In step 3 you work with your team to finalize the scope, project plan, and estimation. This helps build commitment to the plan, and in most cases, the team members reach out to each other and actively solve problems.

In step 4 you involve the team in presenting the project review or gate review to the stakeholders. In order to answer the variety of questions from the stakeholders, it is recommended that you include team members who are knowledgeable in different areas in order to provide the necessary information and to answer questions. Team members will always hold themselves accountable for results when they are involved in planning and presenting to stakeholders. It also raises their visibility and recognition of a job well done.

What are the benefits of involving your team in all four steps of planning the project? They are significant and include

• Commitment and involvement of sponsor and stakeholders to the project, which can increase project success up to 30 percent;
• High sponsor satisfaction with the project, which gets you noticed as a leader;

- A high-quality team, which increases successful outcomes and are more confident and more productive, saving time and money;
- Resolution of problems, risks, and issues, resulting in a project that is 60 percent more effective; and
- Effective decision making during the go/no-go project review with sponsors and stakeholders.

In this chapter I have included the tools and resources to help you focus on your role as communicator and leadership skills to build a high-performing team. Just like project initiation, planning the project will be time intensive, but the effort you put into developing high performing teams is very rewarding.

Let's now begin planning the project. The graph below summarizes the four steps of creating high-performing teams. Across from each step are the required deliverables and the optional resources. These are designed to establish you as the leader of the project and to deliver the project successfully.

CREATING AMAZING TEAMS (Project Planning)		
Step	**Required Deliverables**	**Optional Deliverables**
Step 1: Conduct Planning Meeting	• Kick-off & Planning Meeting Presentation • Scope • Project Plan • Team Expectations Planning Session Deliverables	• Best Practices • Checklist: Project Planning
Step 2: Identify Risk, Communication Plan	• Risk Register • Communication Plan	• Common Project Risks
Step 3: Refine Documents, Project Schedule	• Scope • Project Plan • Estimation	• Project Activity Network Diagram
Step 4: Conduct Project (Gate) Review	• Project (Gate) Review Preparation • Project (Gate) Review Presentation • Project (Gate) Review	• Best Practices • Checklist: Project Planning

Each step has a separate section describing what you need to do. This is an intuitive graphic that allows you to identify at a glance the required and optional deliverables at each step. The remainder of this chapter will discuss each step-in detail. It might be helpful to refer back to this graphic as you read the chapter. We will begin with step 1: conduct planning meeting.

Before we begin, let's look at how David built a high-performing team during the planning meeting.

David's Story: Creating a Productive Project Team

Today, David is conducting the project kickoff and planning meeting. He feels confident that he has prepared a strong presentation, and he came early to set it up. Some team members are in the conference room, and the remaining join the video conference. He scheduled the meeting for eight hours based on the impact of the project to the organization.

Before the meeting begins, a highly respected team member, Susan, comes up to him and asks, "Why do we have an all-day planning meeting? I have so much to do that I cannot afford to spend eight hours in a planning meeting. It is just a waste of time, and I could spend that time so much better. I have been with this company twenty years and worked on many projects, and we never had planning meetings. We just did our tasks."

David could understand why she felt that planning is wasted time. He replied, "Thank you for your feedback. I have found a direct correlation exists between the quality of a project plan and the quality of the execution of the project. Project planning prevents significant rework. On this project, significant conflict between departments has been ongoing for many years. Today, as we go through the planning meeting, I'm confident the team will identify and resolve the conflict among the different departments, and we will have the beginnings of a new and improved process. I have worked with amazing teams, and this team is one of the most skilled and knowledgeable I have had the honor to work with. Susan, at the end of the meeting, could you give me feedback on your observations? I am always looking to find ways to improve."

Susan agreed to provide feedback.

David begins the meeting by reviewing the agenda. Many of the team members know each other, but everyone introduces themselves and their role in the project. After introductions, Ted introduces himself as the sponsor and spends the next ten minutes identifying the importance of the project, what the team needs to accomplish, and his commitment level and support. He answers questions asked by the team and then leaves the meeting. The sponsor does not need to be present while the team is planning the project, as David will provide a summary to Ted later.

David spends the next fifteen minutes defining his expectations for the team members and briefly reviews the methodology that will be used. The real work of the meeting begins with the next topic: review and revise the project scope. David has scheduled four hours for this. The team discusses each item in the scope until they reach agreement.

The team now transitions to developing the project plan. They identified what work needs to be completed in which sequence for everything to flow smoothly. The team sequenced the work in the order it needed to be completed, the key responsibilities of each department, and the impact when work was delivered late to the next department in the sequence.

- Planning department: plans and manages the entire server migration process
- Data center: manages the data center
- Network: manages network-related work
- Implementation: manages server migration and decommission of frame
- Distributed databases: schedules outages and database shutdown, starts checkout
- Server/storage support: works with operations support with cutover (starts the process)
- Operations support: works with server/storage support with cutover (completes the process)

As the team worked together, they realized each department was focused on their own narrow part of the total workflow. Lack of awareness of what other departments did and the impact of delivering their part late had a domino effect. They then identified the necessary coordination. Once each department saw how their work impacted the other departments, they realized they needed to revise the processes.

Everyone now appreciated the work completed by all departments and spent the rest of the meeting revising their processes and sequencing the activities and tasks. Every team member now saw themselves as responsible for the entire process, not just their part. The project team was now fully committed to creating the processes that would make all departments successful. The team leader made arrangements to meet after the planning session to continue to work on the processes and resolve challenges.

By the end of the meeting, the team had identified all the deliverables, activities, activity owners, and activity duration and were excited at what they had created. They were on their way to becoming a high-performing team and felt excited at making positive changes. They identified the need for better communication and came up with a plan, which they implemented that week.

At the end of the meeting, they were so enthusiastic at what they had accomplished that they all clapped for David for the great meeting he had conducted.

After the team members leave, David works with his planner to enter all the information into the electronic project management tool. He then runs a project report with the information and forwards it to the team for review and revision. A few days later, he schedules a second meeting with the team to revise the project management plan, assess project risk, and develop a risk mitigation plan. The team now begins the project work and to complete the activities based on the plan. During the weekly status meetings, David works with his team to identify risks and develop the mitigation plan. The communication plan is being developed by team members.

Once the team has finalized the project plan, communication plan, and risks and the mitigation plan is completed, David prepares for the project or gate review and develops a project review presentation. He then shares the presentation with the team first and then Ted for their review and feedback. David knows how important it is to share the presentation with Ted for final approval before the meeting to maintain his strong partnership and to be recognized as a strong leader. David and his team conduct a practice walk-through before the meeting with the stakeholders. They then present to the stakeholders for a go or no-go decision on the project. The stakeholders respond positively to everything that has been done and give David and the team the go ahead to move into the next phase: execution, monitor, and control.

In project planning, the process of creating amazing teams, David established himself as a strong leader with the sponsor and stakeholders. David also established himself as a strong leader with the project team and is in the process of creating a highly productive, motivated team. He is energized and enthusiastic as he communicates with Ted, the stakeholders, and the team. He always recognizes the contributions of the team to their supervisors, Ted, and the stakeholders.

Step 1: Conduct Planning Meeting

The required deliverables for step 1 are

- Kickoff and planning meeting (presentation)
- Team expectations
- Scope
- Project plan
- Planning session deliverables

The optional deliverables are

- Best practices
- Checklist: project planning

During project planning, you create a high-performing team through the planning process. High-performing teams provide better quality, are responsive, produce work quickly, and have better productivity than is possible for individual performances. These teams have a common vision and goals and partner with each other to achieve outstanding results.

Characteristics of high-performing teams include

- Clear vision of what needs to be accomplished on the project;
- Demonstrating open communication and positive relationship with each other;
- Problem-solving abilities: identify and solve problems;
- Processes to manage conflict;
- Clearly defined roles and work procedures;
- Sharing leadership responsibilities; and
- Having fun working together.

You, the project leader, can take a number of steps to promote high-performing teams:

- Selection of team members who are qualified to complete project tasks and work well on teams;
- Clearly defined project and team objectives. By working together during the planning process, the team identifies the project goals, commits to the goals, and then works cooperatively to accomplish the goals;
- Clearly defined roles and expectations of each team member help provide focus for the project tasks;
- Communication is open and is a priority. Dialog is encouraged;
- Trust is promoted by communication and establishing positive working relationships. Team members treat each other with respect; and
- The team has time for fun. By socializing, celebrating successes, and forming strong relationships with the team members, high-performing teams are created.

Before we discuss step 1, let's spend a few minutes discussing why project planning is so important. There are two main reasons project planning may not happen. First, some organizations do not have the culture or structure to support it. Second, some project managers or teams feel it is a waste of time because it interferes with and unnecessarily delays work on the project. Unfortunately, these beliefs negatively impact project success. There is a direct correlation between a project that is planned by a team working together and the successful delivery of the identified business goals.

In step 1 you conduct the kickoff and planning meeting with your team, using the plans you created in chapter 1. A kickoff meeting is the first meeting with the project team and the client, introducing the members of the project team and the client and providing the opportunity to discuss the role of team members.

How long is a planning meeting? For small projects it may only take an hour or less. For large, complex projects, it may take two to three days. You can use the project sizing tool (phase 1) to help you determine how much time you will need to conduct the meeting.

As the project leader, you facilitate your team working together to gain commitment and to work toward the goals of the project in order to build a high-performing team. The benefits of planning include

- Commitment of sponsor and stakeholder;
- Ability to build a high-performing team:
  - Builds a feeling of camaraderie among the team and they begin working as a team toward the project goal rather than individuals assigned to tasks;
  - Facilitates the sponsor, stakeholders, and team members working in sync toward the same project goal;
- A strong project plan with team planning and involvement;
- A clearly articulated communication plan;
- Risk identification and mitigation processes identified; and
- Clearly identified roles and responsibilities.

Let's begin by looking at how you use the presentation to conduct the kickoff and planning meeting. (Note: you will need to project your presentation onto a screen so it can be seen easily by your team.) In project initiation you prepared the kickoff and planning meeting agenda and presentation. I will now walk you through each slide and provide an explanation of how to present them.

(Supplies needed for meeting: flipchart paper, blue tape to attach the flipchart paper to the walls, Post-It Notes, and different colors of magic markers.)

Conducting the Kickoff and Planning Meeting

Slide: agenda (5–10 minutes)

- Introductions: facilitator, project sponsor, key project/ stakeholders, project manager, team members;
- Conduct project sponsor kickoff with question and answer session;
- Ground rules;
- Identify team expectations;
- Review project management process/methodology that will be used;
- Review and refine project scope document;
- Identify project deliverables;
- Develop project activity network (sticky note exercise); and
- Identify activity owners and estimate activity durations.

Following the planning meeting, the project leader will

- Enter project activity network into project management tool;
- Schedule project and perform schedule compression and determine risk response duration; and
- Generate and distribute activity identification sheet forms.

A few days later, the project leader will schedule a second meeting with the team to

- Review/revise the project management plan; and
- Assess project risk and develop risk response activities.

Open the meeting by reviewing the agenda items. Briefly review each topic so the team knows what will be covered.)

Slide: Introductions (10–15 minutes): facilitator, sponsor, project/stakeholders, project manager, team members

- Sponsor
- Key stakeholders
- Process owner
- Project manager
- Team members
- Customers and vendors

Transition to having each team member introduce themselves. Introduce yourself first with your role as the project manager or leader. After introductions have been made, transition to the next slide.

Conduct project sponsor kickoff with Q&A session (ten to fifteen minutes). Ask the sponsor to review the importance of the project, his or her support for the project, and to open the discussion for a question and answer session. When finished, the sponsor leaves the meeting.

Transition to slide with ground rules, if necessary.

Slide: Ground Rules for Meeting (5 minutes)

- Breaks will occur every 1 to 1.5 hours;
- We will start and resume *on time;*
- One conversation at a time, please;
- Concentrate on what we are doing here, not some other distraction;
- Focus on *what* needs to be done, not *how* to do it; and
- Allow the project manager (person conducting the planning session) to do his or her job without interruption

Review the ground rules you have identified. Ask the team if they would like to include any additional ground rules and add them to your list. Transition to next slide.

Slide: Team expectations for the project (5 minutes)

- Attend status meetings when required (whether in-person or virtual). Attendance is mandatory. If unable to attend, you are expected to update your status before the meeting;
- Update your status weekly via the tool added by the project manager;
- Complete all activities per the schedule that was developed by the team. If you are unable to complete activities per the schedule, immediately notify the project manager;
- Keep calendars updated;
- Identify issues and risks;
- Read all team communication in a timely manner;
- Treat all team members with respect;
- Team to identify escalation process; and
- Project documentation to be stored in a centralized location for easy access.

Review the team expectations and ask if they want to add additional expectations. Generally, I have found teams do not offer additional suggestions. The few minutes it takes to present the team expectations makes a huge difference in the team behavior throughout the project. If you do not identify team expectations, expect to have problems. This is not a failure of the team but of leadership.

Transition to slide: team members. Review and refine project scope document.

- Finalize scope (timeline varies; generally between one and eight hours).

This begins the work of the project. Ask your team to review and revise the first draft of the scope. Generally, this revision will take a minimum of one hour (more likely up to three) for a small project and four to eight hours for longer projects. Do not rush the revision.

The next slide, identify project deliverables and activities, will go fairly smoothly if the scope has been clearly defined.

Example of a Completed Scope Document

Online Low-Cost Storage (OLCS)

Low cost, medium performance, 9x5 support (from 9:00 am to 5:00 pm) has a lower support model from vendor and support staff. It has redundant array of independent disks (RAID) protection. (RAID is a method of storing data on multiple hard disks. When disks are arranged in a RAID configuration, the computer sees them all as one large disk. However, they operate much more efficiently than a single hard drive.)

Use scenarios: closed circuit TV (CCTV), archive data from high-performance computing (HPC), database record archive, desktop services backup data, security hold data (legal hold data- check), scanned records, etc.

Purpose of Project

The purpose of the project is to identify a low-cost storage solution for noncritical data enterprise wide. Some identified noncritical data scenarios are CCTV, archive data from high-performance computing (HPC), database record archive, desktop services backup data, security hold data, (legal hold data-check), scanned records. Currently there is no standard storage solution for noncritical data.

The benefits of the low-cost storage solution include a selection of the most appropriate lowest-cost solution, 9x5 support from the vendor and support staff, and performance and availability equivalent to standard server. Backups will be optional and driven by customer requirements.

A significant benefit of the project is to create low-cost storage standardization industry wide.

Benefits/Opportunity

- **Lower Cost**
  - ○ Less than what tiers 1 and 2 SAN/AS storage costs, but higher than storage on a server.
  - ○ Selection of most appropriate lowest-cost solution Example: Drobo Storage—total cost with three years maintenance under $25,000—with 25 TB usable.
- **Performance**
  - ○ Expected performance is equivalent to standard server.
- **Availability**
  - ○ Expected availability is equivalent to standard server.
- **Support**
  - ○ 9x5 vendor and corporate support team.
- **Backups**
  - ○ Optional—driven by customer requirements.
- **Standardization**
  - ○ Project drives standardization.

Objectives

- Conduct business partner requirement analysis (legal, security, desktop services);
- Research and identify possible solutions;
- Explore and evaluate possible solutions with the use of the Pugh matrix;
- Identify support requirements;
- Reevaluate storage tiers 3 and 4 definitions; and
- Communicate practice.

Project Scope

- ○ **Applications**

- CCTV, archive data from high performance computing (HPC), database record archive, desktop services backup data, security hold data, (legal hold data-check), scanned records.
  - **Location**
    - Regional information center (RIC)
    - Local data centers
    - Remote facilities, depending on customer requirements
  - **Support**
    - 9x5 vendor and corporate support team

Out-of-Scope

List any items that will be specifically excluded from the scope of this project.

- Storage tier 1, tier 2, and tiers 5–9
  - These storage tiers required a higher level of support
- Implementation
- Conducting a formal project

Initial Technical Requirements to be Evaluated

- **Connectivity**
  - SAN, AS, iSCSI
  - If SAN is this SVC storage, brings up supported OS etc.
  - NAS attached best option
  - What about local as a file server? (Server still hosted here)
  - Different functionality between NAS and iSCSI?
- **Data Usage**
  - Is this archived or active? Both

- Transient data (CCTV, desktop imaging)?
- Dormant reports? Yearly reports?
  - ○ **Dynamic Hardware Replacement**
    - Drives and parts hot swap
  - ○ **Dynamic Reconfigurability**
    - Yes (storage side requirement)
  - ○ **Dynamic Capacity Addition**
    - Yes (storage side requirement)
  - ○ **Features**
    - Snap, remote replication
  - ○ **On-Demand Capacity**
  - ○ **Redundant Array of Independent Disks (RAID)**
    - Data protection
    - Yes (RAID 5 w/spare)

Deliverables

1. Define and select standardized solutions;
2. Define enterprise architecture (EA) practice;
3. Train the support team (compile a list as we identify);
4. Redefine tiers 3 and 4 of the storage matrix;
5. Create training documentation; and
6. Conduct a proof of concept (POC).

Note: Create a table with one column titled objectives and one column titled deliverables to make sure the deliverables match the objectives.

Project Budget

Solution has not been identified yet. However, it will be a low-cost solution.

Project Success Indicators

  - ○ Successful completion of the deliverables:

- Define and select standardized solutions;
- Define enterprise architecture (EA) practice;
- Train the support team (compile a list as we identify);
- Redefine tiers 3 and 4 of the storage matrix;
- Create training documentation; and
- Conduct a proof of concept (POC).
  - Ability to implement this storage solution;
  - Lower Cost:
    - Less than what tiers 1 and 2 SAN/NAS storage costs, but higher than storage on a server,
    - Selection of most appropriate lowest-cost solution.

User/Business Unit Impact

- Potential cost savings to enterprise, depending on usage of solution;
- All business units desiring to use the solution:
  - No impact if proper data is in the storage;
    - Impact identified as part of the tiering definition (guideline).

External Dependencies

- Future projects that meet the requirements for the storage solution

Key Project Dates

Identify any key dates that this project will be expected to meet, include driving dates.

Note: Dates set prior to the development of a project schedule are arbitrary and subject to negotiation. Meeting aggressive target dates usually requires reduction in scope, an increase in budget due to additional work or staff resources, and/or a reduction in product quality.

Start Date: February 11
Desired Completion Date: December 20
Other key milestone dates to be determined by the project schedule.
Team Organization
Project sponsor: Kate Thomas
Key stakeholders: Joy Upton, Jake Stone, Emily Reed
Program manager: Qu Won
Project manager: Sue Thon
Team members: Ted New, Sally Say

Constraints

* Cost, specifically the price range of the solution (above)

Risks

* Resource availability

Assumptions

* Will pass the purchased product assessment; and
* Will pass the global purchasing approved supplier process.

Concerns

* Resource availability
* Have necessary equipment to conduct the POC

Glossary

Drobo: A storage company that provides lower-tier storage devices. This will be one of the vendors evaluated as an online low-cost storage (OLCS) provider
RAID: Redundant array of independent disks
Tiers: will be defined during span of project

Congratulations! You have completed revising the scope. You now continue with the remainder of the items on the agenda.

For the remainder of the agenda, you will need supplies: flipchart paper, blue tape (to attach the flipchart paper to the walls; blue tape does not take off the paint), Post-It Notes, and different colored magic markers.

Slide: identify project deliverables and activities (1–6 hours)

- Identify deliverables (one per flipchart):
    - Definition: A list of summary-level sub-products, the delivery of which full and satisfactory marks completion of the project.
- Identify activities for each deliverable on yellow sticky notes (one activity per note):
    - An activity is defined as specific activities (tasks) that must be performed to produce the deliverable.
    - After all activities have been identified for each deliverable, ask the team to place the Post-It Notes for each deliverable in the sequence the activities will be completed.
- Identify activity owners:
    - The owner is defined as the resource who: identifies the resource who will complete the activities, estimated activity duration, guides the resource on completing the activities and reports status to the project leader.
    - The resource is defined as someone who performs the actual work to complete the activity(s).
- Estimate duration of activities; and
- Identify dependencies across all sheets.

Project this slide until the team has completed each item listed on the slide. Facilitate the group so they work together as a team to complete the exercise. Begin by asking your team to identify deliverables and write one on the top of each flipchart. If the team identifies ten, you will have ten flipcharts with one deliverable on each chart. As they write each one on the top of the chart, post it on the wall in the sequence the team thinks each will start.

I've included an example of deliverables for a low-cost electronic storage solution. This example has ten.

1. Determine potential business partners;
2. Determine how business partners will use the solution (voice of the customer);
3. Verify business partner requirements;
4. Develop Pugh matrix (a process to evaluate solutions);
5. Request vendor proposals;
6. Evaluate Pugh matrix and select solution;
7. Conduct proof of concept (POC is documented evidence that a potential product or service can be successful. Developing a POC can help a product owner identify potential technical and logistical issues that might interfere with success);
8. Identify solution;
9. Define tier 3 and 4 storage solutions; and
10. Train support team.

Transition to identify activities for each deliverable (sticky note exercise)

Here is an identify-activities exercise. (An activity is defined as actions that must be performed to produce the deliverable.) Ask your team to identifiy the activities to be completed under each of the deliverables. They write one activity per yellow sticky note and place it under the appropriate deliverable.

Have the team mark the sticky note by drawing a line two inches from the bottom, and and then divide the note below that line into three sections for owner initials, blank center, and duration (see sticky note and flipchart graph below.) Once all the activities for that deliverable have been identified, the team then places the activities in the correct order they will be completed. This process continues until all activities have been listed for each deliverable. Example: above we listed deliverables for a low-cost electronic storage solution. I have identified the activities under two deliverables and in the sequence they must be completed.

- Determine potential business partners (deliverable)

(Activities in the correct sequence)

- – Identify survey participant criteria enterprise wide;
- – Identify survey participants (legal, security, desktop services, engineering, HR);
- – Create the survey; and
- – Send survey to identified biggest users who might be interested.
- Determine how business partners will use the solution (voice of the customer) (deliverable) (activities in the correct sequence)
  - – Analyze the survey results; and
  - – Identify business partner requirements.

Transition to identify activity owners and duration of activities. Ask the team to identify the activity owner for each activity. The activity owners should be part of the project and in the meeting. As the activity owner is identified, they should then identify the duration for those activities.

Transition to identify dependencies across all sheets. Ask the team to identify the dependencies across all the deliverables or charts.

Below is an example of a Post-It Note on the top of the graphic. Below it is a flipchart with all the activities identified. The notes have been sequenced in the order to be completed. This information is then entered into the electronic project tracking tool, where all future work and review of deliverables and activities is completed. You will not need to use the flipcharts again.

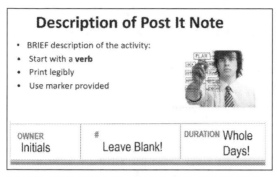

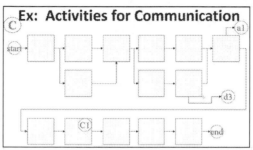

The planning meeting is now completed. You should have the necessary information to enter the information from all the flipcharts into the electronic tracking system. Thank the team for their contributions, and let them know you will enter all the information into the electronic project tracking tool. You will then call a second review meeting in a few days to review and revise the project management plan.

After the meeting, enter the project information into the project management tool. Perform schedule compression and determine risk response duration. Send the team the electronic plan in preparation for the second meeting when they review and revise the project management plan. Schedule a second meeting with the team to review and revise the plan.

- Enter project activity network into project management tool;
- Schedule project and perform schedule compression and determine risk response duration;

- Review/revise the project management plan; and
- Assess project risk and develop risk response activities.

Wow! What a *great* job! You have just completed a lot of work that has helped you create an amazing team.

We are now ready to look at the optional deliverables. They are

- Best practices
- Checklist: project planning

The best practices document covers the practices that your organization follows to promote project success. It's a good idea to review it.

Here is a partial example of a best practices document.

Best Practices

✓ Obtain agreement from sponsor and stakeholders on project objectives and deliverables before starting the project:
   ▪ The sponsor is ultimately responsible for the project achieving business goals;
   ▪ Interview sponsor separately.
✓ Verify how sponsor and stakeholders identify project results and success:
   ▪ Use the scope document to verify this information.
✓ Complete project sizing to identify deliverables and to understand the impact of the project;
✓ Communicate to the sponsor, stakeholders, and your team how you will manage scope, schedule, risk, and communication:
   ▪ Share project management plan; and
   ▪ Present partnership presentation to sponsor.
✓ Build team buy-in and commitment by involving the team in key project decisions:

- Scope document refinement;
- Schedule development:
  - activity ownership
  - duration estimating
  - sequencing
  - resource assignments

✓ Identify what is driving your project's completion date (critical path):
  - Use a fully networked project schedule.

✓ Manage project by duration:
  - Use whole-day durations for all activities.

✓ Plan for the unknown and use risk response time:
  - Place on critical (driving) path prior to key activity/milestone;
  - Minimum 10 percent of project duration.

✓ Understand resource allocation to the project and the non-project responsibilities;

✓ Understand resource availability and impact to the project schedule:
  - Obtain resource availability to work on project from sponsor;
  - Monitor and optimize resource assignments and time reported; and
  - Negotiate with sponsor and stakeholders for agreement on project dates/scope/resources.

✓ Obtain approval of scope from sponsor and stakeholders. Conduct project review before starting the execute, monitor, and control phases.

In project planning there is a checklist to help verify completion of deliverables and activities. Below is an example. It is developed by your organization based on the culture and processes. You should have completed all the activities for step 1.

Sample Checklist: Creating Amazing Teams (Project Planning)

Completed	Step	Activity
Yes	1	Conducted a planning session
Yes	1	Revised project scope
Yes	1	Identified team expectations, standards for team
Yes	1	Identified deliverables, activities, durations, and owners
Yes	1	Entered the project plan into the electronic tracking tool
No	2	Led the team in risk identification and analysis
No	2	Developed a communication plan
No	3	Refined documents and project schedules
No	4	Prepared project review (gate) presentation
No	4	Conducted project (gate) review with your team to sponsor/stakeholders

We are now ready to move to step 2.

Step 2: Identify Risk and Communication Plan

The required deliverables for step 2 are

- Risk register
- Communication plan

The optional deliverable is

- Common project risks

In chapter 1, step 2, we discussed the risk register, a living document that is updated and revised by the team during the life of the project. Let's now look at an example of a completed one. Identifying and resolving risks early significantly increases the success of the project.

This project involved the implementation of tracking software and deals with technical issues.

Completed Risk Assessment

Application: Program for STM monitoring (monitoring software provides STM monitoring)

Servers: Server1.org.com.

Based on the review of the above servers and answers provided, the MySQL team recommends that the databases be migrated to a hardened server and support responsibility for the databases be transferred to the MySQL team. With this solution, the MySQL team would provide a secured, backed up, and monitored server with comparable performance and availability as the current server. The MySQL team would provide 7/24/365 on-call support and assume responsibility for ongoing security compliance. If this proposal is declined, the following is a summary of items that will need to be addressed based on a comparison of the databases against the organizations database technical controls. Continued use of the software will require the submission of a "risk acceptance" by the risk acceptance group.

1. All database passwords comply with the enterprise password strength and expiration requirements. Risk acceptance or customization is required. No passwords are set for root and anonymous user. Password for user of the software does not meet password strength criteria. There was no auditable process identified to track ongoing password compliance.

   Vendor has a patch ready to support non-default software login for MySQL. It is ready to install.

2. A least-privilege required policy is in place:

   a. Only those users who require instance wide/department privileges have them. Risk Acceptance or customization required—all users except anonymous have full privileges.

   b. Application runtime accounts are not granted department access—risk acceptance or customization required. All users except anonymous have full privileges.

Software only requires full privileges for software user on org 1 and org 2 databases.

3. Call-outs are not used. required. The value of local_infile is set to "ON". Call-outs should be disabled by changing the value of local_infile to 0 ("OFF").

   Software needs local_infile to turn on to be able to bulk load data to MySQL database for performance.

   We can send the list of file names that will be used for bulk load. The list can be ready on 9/20/YYYY.

4. The instance hosted on intranet (not in MDZ)—compliant servers on intranet.

5. MySQL "root" account has been renamed and is used only in emergency and should be configured for localhost access ONLY. Risk Acceptance or customization is required. The root account has not been renamed and appears to be actively used. The root account is configured for local access only. The root account does not have passwords set.

   Software only requires root account during initial installation, it does not need root account afterward.

6. MySQL software is a current supported version with recent patches—risk acceptance or customization is required.

   The MySQL version is 5.6.10—enterprise commercial, which is a current acceptable version. Current version for MySQL is 5.5.31 or greater. However, no process to ensure current patches will be applied has been identified.

   Software runs MySQL 5.6.10 enterprise commercial edition.

7. MySQL physical files (both software and database files) have maximum functional protections. Probably not an issue; the MySQL team did not analyze systems for this issue. Securing the files would be the responsibility of the department team.

8. Audit logging is enabled to capture all successful and failed logins, these logs are kept for ninety days—risk acceptance or customization required. All logs are currently turned off. Changing the configuration to enable logging, rotation, and

maintenance of logs would be the responsibility of the department team.

Software has options to turn on/off the logs.

9. Regular database level backups (e.g., myldump or better) are executed and regularly tested to ensure recovery in case of server or media failure. Probably not an issue; the MySQL team did not analyze systems for this issue. The department team would be responsible for backup and recovery of data.

10. Installation scripts, log files and command history files do not contain any passwords or other sensitive information. Probably not an issue; the MySQL team did not analyze systems for this issue. Securing the files would be the responsibility of the department team.

11. There are processes and procedures in place to ensure that all of the above requirements are in control and being reviewed regularly to ensure ongoing compliance. Action required: the department team will be in charge of developing processes and procedures to ensure on-going compliance.

12. The application(s) control and being reviewed regularly to ensure ongoing compliance. Action required: the department team will be in charge of developing processes and procedures to ensure ongoing compliance.

13. The application(s) using this MySQL instance comply with all applicable MySQL license requirements. Compliant department team to verify this MySQL in compliance with open source license.

The next required deliverable is the communication plan, which is required for all projects. It can be quite simple or complex based on the needs of the project. At a minimum, a communication plan needs to contain the following information:

•   What (key message) will be communicated?

- Task (objective)
- Key message
- Who will receive the communication?
  - Owner of the message
  - Communicate to (audience)
- When will it be communicated (times)?
  - Expected start date
  - Actual completion date
- How will it be communicated (meetings, emails, etc.)?
  - Media/resource/activity, etc.

Here is a basic completed communication plan:

COMMUNICATION PLAN

Sponsor Project Request Process

What		Who		When		How
Task (Objective)	Key Message	Owner	Communicate to (Audience)	Expected Start Date	Actual Completion Date	Media/Resource /Activity
High Level Process	Process	Senior Director (J. Stone)	Division Vice President (Amy Lee)	2/20/2018	2/20/2018	1 Slide Presentation
Sponsor Project Request Process	Sponsor Project Request, Governance & Execution Structure Template, Communication Plan	Project Leader (S. Thomas) and Senior Director (J. Stone)	Weekly Staff Meeting	3/5/2018	3/10/2018	Presentation (Stored on Division Shared Drive under PMO / Sponsor Project Request)
Sponsor Project Request Process	Sponsor Project Request, Governance & Execution Structure Template, Communication Plan	Project Leader (S. Thomas) and Senior Director (J. Stone)	Supervisors and Project Requesters	3/5/2018	3/10/2018	Presentation (Stored on Division Shared Drive under PMO / Sponsor Project Request)
GOALS	1) Provide Sponsors / Supervisors a process to submit Project Requests to the department					
	2) Supervisors / Sponsors submit only Projects that have been approved and have funding					
	3) Location of Project Request Template is clearly identified and communicated					

There is one optional but recommended activity. While reviewing and updating the risk register, it is useful to review common project risks prepared by your organization. Examples were provided in section 2.

We are now ready to move to step 3.

Step 3: Refine Documents and Project Schedule

The required deliverables for step 2 are

- Revised scope
- Project plan
- Estimation

The optional deliverable is

- Project activity network diagram

After all the project information (resources, tasks, timelines, etc.) has been entered into the software tracking took, you and your team need to review and update the scope, the project plan, and the estimation for final sign off. The team usually reviews this information a few days after the planning meeting. You and your team adjust these documents to make sure the project plan in the tracking software is up-to-date for the reports you begin generating for your sponsor, stakeholders, team members, and all others.

Optional but recommended is to run a project activity network diagram. If you are using project tracking software in your organization the software should provide network diagrams and most of the software can adjust the reports to meet the needs of the project. This is helpful to use during the project planning phase to ensure sponsor and stakeholders receive all the necessary information. It can also be developed manually on flip chart paper during the planning session. Below is an explanation and information of how to create the network diagram.

Network Diagram Overview

Network diagrams are schematic displays of the project's activities and the logical sequencing (dependencies) among them. Boxes are used to represent the activities and arrows are drawn to show the dependencies. Accurate sequencing of activities is crucial to developing realistic and achievable schedules.

An approach that works well to complete the development:

- The team needs to review and validate the relationships for the project;
- When building the network, identify the connections between tasks within the deliverables; and
- Include milestones, known dependencies to other projects, and activities detailed in the project management plan.

Dependency Types

- Finish to start (FS): An activity must finish before the next activity can start;
- Start to start (SS): Activities that start at the same time; and
- Finish to finish (FF): Activities that finish at the same time.

The planning phase is now completed and all documents updated. Your next step is to prepare to present the plan to your sponsor and stakeholders for the go/no-go decision on the project.

Step 4: Conduct Project (Gate) Review

The required deliverables for step 2 are

- Prep for project (gate) review
- Create presentation for project (gate) review
- Conduct project (gate) review meeting with sponsor/ stakeholders

The optional deliverables are

- Best practices
- Checklist: project planning

You prepare for the review by making sure all the activities and deliverables have been completed and approved. I compiled a list below of required deliverables to help you in the process. If you have not completed all the items, complete them before moving forward. This list should be customized for your project.

Project Review #1 Preparation

(Have all these deliverables been shared with the sponsor?)
- Partnered with sponsor
- Scope document approved
- Project plan completed
- Communication plan developed
- Project sizing tool completed
- Schedule complete (tasks, resources, activities)
- Cost estimate complete
- Risk register and issue log up-to-date
- Test strategy identified
- Implementation strategy identified

You are now ready to prepare the project (gate) #1 review presentation. All the information should be summarized and presented. You prepare the presentation and then review it with your team. It is also important to share your presentation with your sponsor before the meeting with the stakeholders to make sure you are working as partners. It can be uncomfortable and embarrassing if your sponsor is in disagreement or angry with your presentation.

At the end of the presentation, the stakeholders make a go or no-go decision whether the project should continue and move to the execute, monitor, and control phase. Below are general guidelines you can follow as you prepare for the project (gate) review for sponsors and stakeholders. It may take a considerable amount of time to develop the presentation because it needs to be concise and the meeting lasts no longer than half an hour. Being concise takes time.

By following the recommendations in the first two chapters, you should now have established a strong, positive working relationship with your sponsor and have earned their respect for you as a leader.

Project (Gate) #1 Review Guidelines

The purpose of the first review is to provide a structured approach to ensure projects meet business objectives with appropriate quality.

- Enhanced project performance
  - ✓ Ensure projects have necessary resources before continuing, reducing delays and optimizing project performance.
- Improved delivery quality
  - ✓ Ensure necessary work is completed before advancing: Increasing deliverable quality, improving delivery and reducing costly rework.
- Improved communication and alignment
  - ✓ Reviews include business partners to provide updated estimates and ensure alignment of delivery expectations and outcomes.

Project Review Guiding Principles

- Need to be flexible to account for varying sizes and complexities of projects, as well as different methodologies;
- Provide value-add governance to support business objectives;
- Projects where the requirements have not been met will be stopped from proceeding until the expectations of the project review are met; and
- A project cannot proceed without a go decision by the project key stakeholders for the specific review.

Project Review Process

Criteria to Conduct Review (Gate) Meeting
- Required deliverables have been completed;
- Project manager can answer yes to all expectations or can explain deviations;
- Deviations are documented for distribution to key stakeholders prior to the meeting; and
- Project manager scheduled the review meeting and routes the project scope document.

Project (Gate) Review Meeting

- Team created required deliverables;
- Major issues, risks, deviations, and variances are discussed;
- Sponsor and stakeholders determine whether project should
  - ➢ Proceed
  - ➢ Pause for rework (requires a follow-up review)
  - ➢ Be stopped
- Decide when next review (gate) should occur; and
- Document deficiencies and corresponding remediation steps.

Exit Criteria

- Review decision is documented on project review template;
- Next project (gate) review is scheduled (included in project schedule); and
- Follow-up project (gate) review is scheduled if project is paused for rework.

Timing for Project (Gate) Review 1

- Happens prior to starting execute monitor control
  - ✓ Can be done at the same time as obtaining project scope document approval.

- Review expectations include
  - ✓ Project scope document—has been or ready for approval;
  - ✓ Project schedule complete—fully networked and ready to baseline;
  - ✓ Cost estimate—detailed estimate complete;
  - ✓ Resource allocation—entered for each resource and planned use is in line with their allocation percentage; and
  - ✓ Risk register, issue and scope change logs—up-to-date and key items prepared for review, as needed.

Recommended Items to Present

- Gate review document
- Key points from project scope document
- Major risks
- Known issues
- Any of the gate review deliverables
  - ✓ Can vary based on input from sponsor/key stakeholder

Participants

- Project sponsor
- Key stakeholders/business partner
  - ✓ Key stakeholders are any person or organization that can significantly impact or be impacted by the results of the project
- Project manager
- Team members
- Architect, as needed (based on deliverables, e.g., technical design)
- Others as needed

Format

- Varies by project—virtual, conference call, or in-person based on key stakeholder locations; and

- For small-sized projects where all review expectations are met and no outstanding issues/risks remain, key stakeholders can provide authorization to proceed on review template via email—no review meeting required.

Duration

- One hour or less

Strong Recommendation

- Review the presentation with the sponsor before sharing with the stakeholders to ensure the sponsor is fully aware of what you will present;
- This will eliminate surprises and miscommunication.

We are now ready to discuss the optional deliverables.

- Best practices
- Checklist: project planning

Review the best practices document by your organization. This will help ensure you can fully answer the stakeholders' questions. It is another useful tool to ensure that those practices are followed that will help achieve success.

A quick review of the checklist for project planning helps you verify that all the steps and deliverables have been completed.

Sample Checklist: Creating Amazing Teams (Project Planning)

Completed	Step	Activity
Yes	1	Conducted a planning session
Yes	1	Revised project scope
Yes	1	Identified team expectations, standards for team

Yes	1	Identified deliverables, activities, durations, and owners
Yes	1	Entered the project plan into the electronic tracking tool
Yes	2	Led the team in risk identification and analysis
Yes	2	Developed a communication plan
Yes	3	Refined documents and project schedules
Yes	4	Prepared project review (gate) presentation
Yes	4	Conducted project (gate) review with sponsor/ stakeholders

You are amazing! You have created a foundation of success and an amazing team for your project. You are now ready to begin executing the project plan or tasks and delivering project success.

Delivering Project Success
(Execute, Monitor, Control)

CONGRATULATIONS! YOU HAVE created a strong working partnership with the sponsors and stakeholders, you have developed a highly productive team, the project plan has been developed jointly by you and the team, and a risk mitigation process has been implemented. You are communicating frequently with the sponsor and stakeholders, the team and all others involved in the project. At the project (gate) review you received the go decision to move forward with the project. The foundation for success and your awesome project team will now help you deliver project success.

You are now ready to deliver project success by completing the work and delivering the business goals. As the team begins work on the activities and tasks, you provide status reports and updates to the sponsor and stakeholders. Because you are using technology to manage the tactical information, you are able to focus on value-add activities of communication, your partnership with the sponsor and stakeholders, mitigating risks, and leading the team.

There are four steps to execute, monitor, and control in order to deliver project success. Unlike the steps during project initiation and planning, which are done sequentially, these four steps are done simultaneously. In execute, monitor, and control, the project schedule is executed per the project plan. You track any changes or variances to the project and share with the sponsor. You and your team update documents that were prepared in the first two phases. The four steps provide detailed information, tools, and resources to help you deliver the project successfully.

In step 1, you update status reports and work with your team to make sure the project stays on track. In step 2, you update your sponsor and stakeholders by providing requested status reports and presentations. In step 3, you update the scope, risk documents, and communication plan and create change requests if needed to keep your sponsor and stakeholders updated. In steps 1–4, the project schedule is executed per the plan. You track any changes or variances and share with the sponsor.

The project will be successful because

- You have built a strong foundation for success so the project moves forward as planned;
- The amazing team you have created delivers results per the project plan;
- The project results meet sponsor and stakeholder expectations; and
- You deliver on time and within budget.

Let's now begin execute, monitor, and control to deliver the project successfully. The graph below summarizes the four steps for delivering the project successfully. Across from each step are the required deliverables and the optional resources. Use your leadership to guide your team to deliver the project successfully.

Each step has a separate section describing what you need to do. This is an intuitive graphic that allows you to identify at a glance the required and optional deliverables at each step. The remainder of this chapter will discuss each step of execute, monitor, and control in detail. It might be helpful to refer back to this graphic as you read the chapter.

	DELIVERING PROJECT SUCCESS (Execute, Monitor, Control)	
Step	**Required Deliverables**	**Optional Deliverables**
Step 1: Provide Status Reports	• Status Reports	• Checklist: Execute, Monitor, Control
Step 2: Update Sponsor/ Stakeholders	• Status Reports • Sponsor/Stakeholder Presentations	• Cause of Schedule Variance • Glide Paths
Step 3: Execute Scope, Communication, Manage Risk	• Scope • Risk Register • Issue Log • Change Request • Communication Plan	• Project Activity Network Diagram • Pugh Matrix (if applicable)
Step 4: Execute Project Schedule	• Manage Schedule in Tracking Tool	• Best Practices • Checklist: Execute, Monitor, Control

David's Story—Delivering Project Success

David and the team are energized at the positive response from the stakeholders at the gate review and immediately begin to enthusiastically work on the project. They complete the activities and update the status of their tasks weekly via the electronic tracking tool. David manages the project through status reports. The team reviews the risks and mitigation plan weekly. The communication plan is being followed. The plan is managed via the project tracking tool, and adjustments are made as necessary.

David has scheduled the weekly thirty-minute status update meetings on Ted's calendar through the end of the project. Ted had requested these meetings when David shared the partnership presentation in project initiation. Each week he prepares two summary slides to share with Ted.

The project is moving along very smoothly. The team is motivated to make the project a success and work proactively together to resolve risks. For the first time in years, all the team leads in each department are working together and understand the challenges faced by each department. Now that they are in execute, monitor, and control, where the team completes the activities and tasks, David has much less work to do and spends most of his time communicating with Ted, the stakeholders, and the team.

Once the tasks of the execute, monitor, and control are about three-fourths completed, David prepares for gate review #2 to review the project again with the stakeholders. He again follows the same procedure as before with sponsor and team and then presents to the stakeholders.

Throughout the project, David has established himself as a strong leader. He has created a highly productive, motivated team and frequently acknowledges their contributions. He is energized and enthusiastic as he and the team deliver project success.

Step 1: Provide Status Reports

The required deliverables for step 1:

- Team provides regular updates (usually electronic)
- Status reports

The optional deliverable is

- Checklist: Execute, Monitor, Control

The project is underway, and you are now ready to keep it together and move forward. How will you know if people are doing what they promised? How can you meet your objectives and still get everything done?

You see how your leadership skills have helped build a strong foundation and highly productive team. The team is now relying on your leadership to help them successfully complete the project.

Begin by setting up a schedule for your team to report the status of their tasks. The team agreed to update the status weekly per the expectations identified in the kickoff meeting. The most efficient and preferred method is to have each team member update the status of his or her assigned tasks directly into the software tracking tool. Project tracking software can now electronically generate customized status reports in minutes, showing the current status (if the information is maintained and updated).

The main benefit of technology is the significant time saved by your team over the life of the project. Team members can spend 10-15 minutes per week logging into the site at their desk and updating the tasks. If they attend a project meeting, they often waste time because much of the meeting doesn't apply to them. You strengthen your role as a leader by respecting and protecting the time of your team by streamlining the task-reporting process, allowing them to focus on completing the tasks rather than attending meetings.

Using technology frees you up to focus on value-add skills of communication and risk mitigation. Resolving risks early helps ensure success of the project. Use the meetings to identify deviations from the project plan and identify actions to keep the project on track. By drawing out and utilizing the skills of your team, you will be amazed at what they can accomplish.

By completing the above steps, you will be able to accurately communicate the progress and status of your project to leaders and all others involved in the project. You will be able to run a wide variety of electronic status reports to fit the need of your audience. During project initiation you worked with your sponsor to identify the type of reports that meet their need. At this point in execute, monitor and control, you are now ready to provide these reports to your sponsor.

The most useful status report for your sponsor and stakeholders is the one-page summary status report. It can be shared weekly, biweekly, monthly, or on demand with your leaders. It includes

- Upper right corner: the project health (overall, scope, schedule, budget and resources);
- The percentage complete for the project;
- Center of the report: a timeline of the key deliverables and the status of each. A green checkmark indicates it has been completed; and
- The bottom of the report: key accomplishments and items for awareness.

A second example is again one page, but it includes milestones and the status of each. Depending on the software you are using, you may need to enter information manually. This again is useful for leaders to see at a quick view the progress of the project.

This report shows

- Milestones and the status of each;
- Key activities planned for next week;
- Issue and risks;
- Key achievements; and
- Key activities planned for the following week.

Both examples are shown below.

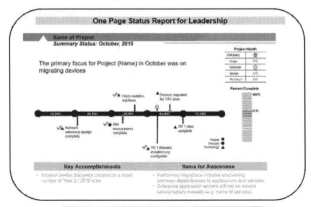

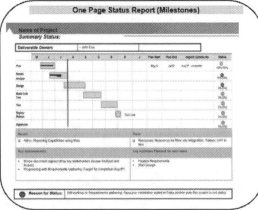

We have just looked at project status reports for individual projects. Let's now look at a status report for multiple projects. In most organizations, there is often a portfolio of active projects, all at different phases. Leaders need a status report providing an overview of all these projects.

What is a portfolio status report or a summary status report of multiple projects? It is a report created in a database that contains both a one-page summary dashboard and tabs for individual status reports and can be accessed 24/7 by the project team and leaders. As the individual status reports are completed manually by the project manager, the dashboard is populated automatically. Leadership uses the dashboard to review a range of projects within a division, department, or across divisions or departments. A summary dashboard contains all the critical information needed by leadership to understand each project.

Dashboard Summary Page

- Project name
- Supervisor or division manager
- Project manager
- Overall status (color coded: green, yellow, red)
- Project status (color coded: not started, planning, in process)
- Percent complete
- Project plan complete (color coded: green, yellow, red)
- Scope complete (color coded: green, yellow, red)
- Glide path
- Open issues
- Start date
- End date
- Projects listed on the bottom of the report are also color coded (red, yellow, blue = completed, gray = on hold)

The individual status reports are completed weekly or monthly by the project manager.

Individual Status Reports

- Information on team members, sponsors
- Project health based on eight categories (color coded: red, yellow, green)
- Key accomplishments and steps planned for next reporting period
- Issues and risks
- Milestones and program phase

You are now ready to complete the one optional deliverable. It is a highly recommended activity. It is to review the checklist for execute, monitor and control. This helps you as the project leader prepare to complete all required steps during the execute, monitor and control phase of the project. Note that this checklist is different from the previous two. All the activities listed are completed throughout the entire phase and not only during a specific step.

Below is the list of activities that are expected of you as the project leader during the execute, monitor, control phase. Because you have established yourself as the leader and have created a high-performing team, you are now well positioned to fulfill the following responsibilities. Again, you will need to complete all four steps of execute, monitor, control at the same time, so the checklist reflects this.

Sample Checklist: Phase 3: Delivering Project Success (Execute, Monitor, Control)

Completed	Steps	Activity
Yes	1–4	Conducted regular status meetings
Yes	1–4	Gathered and utilized team members' activity status to update schedule
Yes	1–4	Provided regular updates to the sponsor and stakeholders
Yes	1–4	Involved team members in schedule compression

Yes	1–4	Communicated project status on schedule and budget
Yes	1–4	Managed issues, risks and scope change requests
Yes	1–4	Encouraged/solicited participation from all activity owners
Yes	1–4	Updated documents (scope, risk register, communication plan)
Yes	1–4	Demonstrated proactive risk management
Yes	1–4	Effectively led the team toward achieving desired project outcome
Yes	1–4	Demonstrated effective problem solving/troubleshooting
Yes	1–4	Dealt with personality conflict before they impacted performance
Yes	1–4	Utilized the skills, capabilities, and experiences of team members
Yes	1–4	Was open and accessible to team members
Yes	1–4	Was well organized
Yes	1–4	Demonstrated good written communication skills
Yes	1–4	Gained project team members' buy-in through active listening and relationship building
Yes	1–4	Worked well with others
Yes	1–4	Demonstrated good oral communications
Yes	1–4	Demonstrated timeliness (attendance, punctuality, fulfillment of obligations), accuracy, and thoroughness in working project activities
Yes	1–4	Initiated change requests as needed
Yes	1–4	Conducted all project reviews
Yes	1–4	Managed schedule in electronic tracking tool

Step 2: Update Sponsor and Stakeholders

The required deliverables for step 2 are

- Customized status reports for leaders as requested
- Sponsor/stakeholder presentation

The optional deliverables are

- Cause of schedule variance
- Glide paths

As you move through the project, often your sponsor or stakeholders may require customized status reports. They are most interested in on-time delivery, cost, risks and use of resources. If you and your team are updating the tasks on a weekly basis, you will be able to provide these reports easily, quickly, and efficiently. Most of the time you can run these reports within minutes. At other times you may need to do a combination of electronic reports and manual entry into the status report.

During project initiation, you met with your sponsor to identify frequency of update meetings. For each of these meetings it is recommended that you prepare a short presentation with graphics to share with your sponsor. These meetings generally are short if the project is moving along well and can last from fifteen minutes to half an hour. If there are challenges, the meetings will take longer as you need to resolve the challenges. Again, I am emphasizing the importance of frequent and regular communication with the sponsor for project success.

In addition to regular update meetings with your sponsor, you will also need to present project updates to your stakeholders. These updates are usually more formal project (gate) reviews. You already presented a project (gate) review #1 at the end of project planning, creating amazing teams, where the stakeholders gave you the Go decision to move to the execution, monitor, and control where the project plan is completed. You will now present review #2 to the stakeholders.

Project review #2 is usually conducted when the execute, monitor, and control tasks are about three-fourths completed. The purpose can be to review whether the project is ready to complete the execution stage. Is rework required? Perhaps there is significant variance from the original plan. Or, and the best reason, just to update the stakeholders that the project is moving along per the project plan. Below are guidelines for project (gate) review #2.

Project (Gate) #2 Review Guidelines

Timing

- The second project (gate) review occurs before key project events such as roll out, go live, etc.;
- Also schedule reviews if
  - There is significant cost/scope/schedule changes; and
  - The stakeholders desire a meeting.
    - Key stakeholders may decide additional gate reviews are desirable prior to gate 2, depending on project duration, risk, methodologies, or other factors.

Review #2

- Happens prior to project's key event (go-live, implementation, deploy, etc.).
  - ✓ Can be done at the same time as obtaining project scope document approval.
- Review expectations:
  - ✓ Go-live criteria met—what business partners agree needs to be ready before go live.
  - ✓ Project costs and schedule are up-to-date and within commitments made in the current project scope document.
  - ✓ Backout plan is complete.
  - ✓ Risk register, issue, and scope change logs are up-to-date, and key items are prepared to review as necessary.

Additional Reviews

- Key stakeholders may request additional reviews:
  - ✓ Based on methodology (e.g., six sigma, AQA, Agile, etc.);
  - ✓ Based on project's schedule (if project (gate) review is several monthss in the future);
  - ✓ Based on project's risk and/or visibility; and
- If current gate deliverable is not approved and needs to be reworked.

Meeting Structure

- Purpose: Assess the project's preparedness to continue.

Participants

- Project sponsor
- Key stakeholders (business partner)
- Project manager
- Architect, as needed (based on deliverables, such as technical design)
- Others, as needed

Format

- Varies by project: virtual, conference call, or in-person based on kley stakeholder locations.
- For small-sized projects where all review expectations are met and no outstanding issues/risks, key stakeholders can provide authorization to proceed on review template via email; no review meeting required.

Duration

- One hour or less

You have now completed the required deliverables for step 2. There are two optional deliverables that are also useful. A form to identify cause of schedule variance can help provide consistency in how you identify and analyze schedule variances. It occurs in most projects for any number of reasons. It is important is to identify and determine what to do about it. An effective process is to work with your team during the status meetings to identify the reasons variance is occurring and what to do about it.

Record schedule variance analysis on a form that includes the following information:

- Cause of schedule variance
- Variance amount in days
- Date slippage was identified
- New scheduled project completion date.

An additional useful tool is the glide path, which can be helpful for deployment, IT projects, large training initiatives, etc. The data is entered into a database that generates the glide path. It provides a quick check that all activities and deliverables have been completed. It is a line and bar chart showing completion.

Step 3: Execute Scope, Communication, Risk Management

The required deliverables for step 2 are to update the

- Scope
- Risk register
- Issue log
- Communication plan
- Change request

The optional deliverables are

- Project activity network diagram
- Pugh matrix

As discussed in the introduction, if you have established yourself as the leader, you will find the execution, monitor, and control, delivering project success, enjoyable and energizing for your team. Let's take a look at why your leadership skills help to energize your team. Below are a few of the leadership skills required of a project leader.

Effectively lead your team toward achieving desired project outcome. Following the processes and steps identified in this book will enable you to lead your team toward achieving the business objectives of the project.

Deal with personality conflict before they impact performance. Resolving personality conflicts to help your team work together effectively is expected of you as the project leader. Trust in you as a leader facilitates the resolution of conflicts.

Gain project team members' buy-in through active listening and relationship building. By practicing listening and relationship building when the project is assigned to you, and demonstrating these skills during the kickoff and planning meeting, shows that you are a leader with these skills. As a result, your team trusts and respects you.

Utilize the skills, capabilities, and experiences of team members. As a leader, you are able to draw out and expand your team members' capabilities, providing new opportunities and recognizing their growth and accomplishments. This will increase the loyalty of your team and enhance your reputation as a leader.

During this step, you are updating and revising existing documents created during project initiation and planning. Working with your team you update the following documents to keep the project current. All these documents should be stored in a central database accessible to all team members:

- Scope
- Risk register
- Change request
- Communication plan

If there are any change requests involved with your project, you will need to create a change request document. It is used when changes occur to the project schedule, cost and scope. This helps you manage the changes and to implement only approved changes. The process includes the following functions:

- Recognize items that fall outside of or which represent changes to the approved scope of the project;
- Analyze and document the impact of these requests;
- Assess the business value of the requests to make informed decisions whether they should be incorporated, denied, or deferred to a subsequent project;
- Require formal approval from sponsor and key stakeholders before the change is incorporated into the project effort for changes that modify previously documented scope definitions or cause project to exceed cost or date thresholds previously identified; and
- Capture and publicize the disposition of change requests to ensure all parties are aware of the status of all requests.

Usually a change requester is assigned to the project and will work with you to determine whether the desired feature/function currently exists, has a workaround, or needs to be submitted as a change request.

- Once the initial information is captured, you as the project leader decide whether the request will be processed as a change request.
- You record the project sponsor and key stakeholders' decision on the change request register and informs the requester of the decision.

If the change is accepted, you update the project scope document and adjust the project schedule to reflect the change (activities, relationships, and dates). It is also a good idea to present the project scope to your sponsor and key stakeholders for sign-off on the changes. After the change has been completed, it is your role as project leader to document them on a form developed by the organization.

There are two optional activities. The project activity network diagram was discussed in chapter 2, step 3 under optional deliverables, project activity network diagram. It is a useful approach at this point in the project to review it for project accuracy. Network diagrams are schematic displays of the project's activities and the logical sequencing (dependencies) among them. Boxes are used to represent the activities and arrows are drawn to show the dependencies. Accurate sequencing of activities is crucial to developing realistic and achievable schedules. You should be able to print these reports electronically from the project tracking tool.

The next optional activity is the Pugh matrix (if applicable). The Pugh matrix is typically used by a team to evaluate potential solutions and then select the best based on the selection process. It is extremely helpful in making decisions and clarifying what is most important.

Following is a description of the tool and how to use it.

Pugh Matrix Guidelines

- Used to facilitate a team-based process for concept generation and selection;
- Helps determine which items or potential solutions are more important or better than others;
- Should be done after capturing the voice of the customer (VOC); and
- A scoring tool used for concept selection, in which options are assigned scores relative to criteria.

Developed by

- Evaluating several concepts according to their strengths and weaknesses against a base concept (DATUM) until an optimal concept finally is reached.

Steps for Concept Selection

- Define concepts/solutions
- Identify key criteria

- Determine relative importance ratings
- Select DATUM (base concept)
- Compare each of the alternative concepts against the DATUM
  - Using clearly better: "+"
  - Clearly worse: "-"
  - About the same: "s"
- Sum the (+)s, (-)s, and (s)s
- Look for strengths and weaknesses; attack and eliminate the weaknesses
- Complete configuration run
  - Using the strongest concept as the DATUM
- If the second run confirms the first, this would be your selected concept.

Note: If you find more than one strong concept/solution, you may need to reevaluate your key criteria and concepts.

Description of PUGH Matrix Form (Excel)
Ratings Columns in the Following Order from Left to Right: Criteria

- Importance rating (5 = high, 0 = low)
- DATUM (best current concept at each iteration)
- Concept 1
- Concept 2
- Concept 3
- Concept 4
- Etc.

Calculations Columns: New Section at the Bottom of the Pages

- Sum of positives
- Sum of negatives
- Sum of sames
- Weighted sum of positives
- Weighted sum of negatives

Let's look at an example where the Pugh matrix was used to decide which car to buy.

Examle: Buying a Car

Explanation of form for this example. It consists of five columns:

1. Rating criteria (explained above)
2. DATUM
3. Concept 1
4. Concept 2
5. Concept 3

Rating Criteria

- 4-wheel drive
- Design style
- Price
- Warranty
- Relate value
- Color
- Interior room
- Navigation system
- Reliability

DATUM

- Jeep Wrangler

Concept 1

- Nissan Murano

Concept 2

- Infiniti FX35

Concept 3

- VW Tuareg

Each car is then rated from one to five against the Jeep Wrangler based on the criteria, and the results are then calculated. It is recommended that this process be repeated at least twice. Often a different DATUM is used for the second rating.

Purpose of Confirmation Run

- First-run outcome may be a result of personal favorites as opposed to best choice; and
- Ensures that the "best" selection is based on facts as opposed to personal emotions.

Steps 1–4: Execute Project Schedule

The required deliverable

- Manage schedule in tracking tool

The optional deliverables are

- Best practices
- Checklist: execute, monitor, control

Managing the project schedule in the tracking tool is necessary to provide accurate, up-to-date information on the project. In many organizations, a planner is assigned to manage the updates, tasks, etc. in the tracking tool. This is optimal and allows you as the project leader to focus on communication, risk mitigation, and variance. By analyzing the reports, you can determine the health of the project, guide the progress of your team, and identify work still to be done.

You use your leadership skills fully during this phase. As the project leader, good negotiation skills are needed to navigate the political waters that can slow down a project or stop it entirely. The partnership you have built with the sponsor will help you navigate these challenges. The processes you have put in place during project initiation and planning ensure that the work is done at the right time and in the right sequence. You have selected team members who have the necessary knowledge and expertise to complete the activities and tasks on schedule. And you are using technology to manage your project.

As the project leader, you understand and communicate

- Outcomes of activities;
- What has been done/not done;
- Extent to which quality standards are being met;
- Additional costs that have been committed;
- Expenditures that have been made to date;
- Actual date items began and ended;
- Actual hours expended on work to date; and
- Projected hours to complete schedule work (revised estimations).

Status meetings are conducted to identify variance and risk mitigation and to ensure the project is on track for successful completion.

Examples of agenda items can include

- Activities and tasks that are behind schedule, the impact, and approaches to get back on track;
- Review or summary of approved change requests that impact the team members;
- Review of risks and mitigation plans and progress;
- Any issues; and
- Action plans.

Project risk must be continuously monitored and managed throughout the project with you team usually during status meetings. The risk register or any other useful tool can be used.

- Ensure that the risk responses have been implemented as planned;
- Evaluate whether risk responses are effective as planned or need to be revised;
- Ensure assumptions are still valid;
- Ensure that policies and procedures are being followed; and
- Identify, analyze, and plan responses for any new risks.

Two optional tools that help you manage the project are best practices and the checklist for the execute, monitor, control phase.

Use the checklist to evaluate yourself as a project leader.

Sample Checklist: Delivering Project Success (Execute, Monitor, Control)

Completed	Steps	Activity
Yes	1–4	Conducted regular status meetings
Yes	1–4	Gathered and utilized team members' activity status to update schedule
Yes	1–4	Provided regular updates to the sponsor and stakeholders
Yes	1–4	Involved team members in schedule compression
Yes	1–4	Communicated project status on schedule and budget
Yes	1–4	Managed issues, risks, and scope change requests
Yes	1–4	Encouraged/solicited participation from all activity owners
Yes	1–4	Updated documents (scope, risk register, communication plan)
Yes	1–4	Demonstrated proactive risk management
Yes	1–4	Effectively led the team toward achieving desired project outcome

Yes	1–4	Demonstrated effective problem solving/ trouble shooting
Yes	1–4	Dealt with personality conflicts before they impacted performance
Yes	1–4	Utilized the skills, capabilities, and experiences of team members
Yes	1–4	Was open and accessible to team members
Yes	1–4	Was well organized
Yes	1–4	Demonstrated good written communication skills
Yes	1–4	Gained project team members' buy-in through active listening and relationship building
Yes	1–4	Worked well with others
Yes	1–4	Demonstrated good oral communications
Yes	1–4	Demonstrated timeliness (attendance, punctuality, fulfillment of obligations), accuracy, and thoroughness in working project activities
Yes	1–4	Initiated change requests as needed
Yes	1–4	Conducted all project reviews
Yes	1–4	Managed schedule in electronic tracking tool

Celebrating Success (Project Close)

WHAT AN ACCOMPLISHMENT! You built a foundation for success, a high performing team and that in turn led you to deliver the business goals and project success that met or exceeded the expectations of the sponsor and stakeholders. Unlike project initiation, project planning, and execute, monitor, and control, project close is usually completed quickly.

Based on your successes above, you are now ready to close the project and reap the benefits of work well done. There are four steps to project close. In step 1, you organize the final project documentation in an archive site that can be easily used as a reference for future projects. In step 2, you conduct a project close meeting with your team. In step 3 you communicate the project close to all parties. And in step 4, you archive the project and celebrate with your team. Share the success with leaders and others and express interest in new, challenging opportunities to your manager, sponsor, and stakeholders. You are now ready to celebrate success.

The benefits include

- Increased confidence of assuming new and challenging opportunities;
- Expanded leadership skills;

- Respect from your project team, who will support you in your career; and
- Creation of a project team that had fun working together and exceeded sponsor and stakeholder expectations.

Let's begin project close, celebrating success. The graph below summarizes the four steps of closing the project. Across from each step are the required deliverables and the optional resources. Use your leadership to guide your team to close the project successfully.

Each step has a separate section describing what you need to do. This is an intuitive graphic that allows you to identify at a glance the required and optional deliverables at each step. The remainder of this chapter will discuss each step-in detail. It might be helpful to refer back to this graphic as you read the chapter.

ACCELERATING YOUR CAREER (Project Close)		
Step	**Required Deliverables**	**Optional Deliverables**
Step 1: Organizes Final Documentation	• Status Reports • Project Documentation • Project Closed in Tracking Software	• Checklist: Project Close
Step 2: Conduct Project Close Meeting	• Lessons Learned • Project Completion Report	• Project Manager Feedback • Team Member Feedback
Step 3: Communicate Project Close	• Communication	• Compare Projects
Step 4: Project Closed	• Archive Project • Team Celebration	• Communicate Success with Leaders

David's Story—Celebrating Success

David has delivered the project successfully. Ted and the stakeholders are very pleased with the result. For the first time in years, the departments are working well together, communicating frequently, and checking in with each other. The mood among the team and departments is one of success and a job well done. The project team love working with David and have asked to worked on any future projects he leads. Ted has been talking to David about his career and what he would like to do. David tells him he would like to move into a leadership position, and Ted has started mentoring him.

To close out the project, David reviews all the documentation that he has placed in archives to make sure it is complete. The planner closes the project in the tracking software. David schedules one last meeting with the project team to discuss lessons learned and to complete the project completion report. The team discusses how they will celebrate their success and come up with a plan.

After the meeting, David places the two reports in the archive file. He then sends communication to all parties that the project has been completed and is closed. He lets everyone know where they can access the archived files. The next week the team celebrates their success.

David has made a positive impact on the organization and enhanced the functioning of the departments that were involved. Everyone recognizes his contribution. David is very proud of his team for their amazing performance and communicates this to their managers. David loves his job and coming to work every day. He knows he is making valuable contributions to the success of his organization.

Step 1: Organize Final Documentation

The required deliverables are

- Status reports
- Project documentation
- Project closed in tracking software

The optional deliverables are

- Checklist: project close

Now that the project has been completed, you organize all the documentation in a project archive data, following the organization's guidelines and process. This information should be easily accessed and used as reference for future projects. At the minimum, the following should be organized:

- By dates: status reports from the start of the project to the end;
- By dates: stakeholder update meetings including the presentations and other documentation;
- Final scope document;
- Risk register and risk worksheet;
- Change plans; and
- All other documentation that was part of the project, including vendor contracts, etc.

You will also want to close the project in the tracking software. Verify that all tasks and activities have been closed and the costs recorded per your organization. The project is then closed and archived so no additional updates or changes can be made.

This is optional, but a review of the checklist for project close is a quick reminder of what you need to do to close the project.

Sample Checklist: Celebrating Success (Execute, Monitor, Control)

Completed	Steps	Activity
Yes	1	Organized and archived all project documentation
Yes	1–4	Successfully led the project
No	2	Conducted project close
No	2	Involved the team in documenting lessons learned for the project
No	3	Communicated project close
No	4	Project closed

Step 2: Conduct Project Close Meeting

The required deliverables are

- Lessons learned
- Project completion report

The optional deliverables are:

- Project manager feedback
- Team member feedback

Conducting a lessons learned meeting with the team is a way to celebrate all the successes and to identify ways to make the projects even more successful in the future. Conduct a meeting with your project team to discuss lessons learned and to formally close the project with the team. Ask your team to review project initiation, project planning, execute, monitor, and control, and project close. For each phase, discuss and record on a form

- Lessons learned;
- What worked and why;
- What would you do differently and why;
- Major project strengths; and
- Major project weaknesses.

At the same meeting, also complete the project completion report with your team. This report includes information on project results, successes, variances, changes, and other observations. Attach the lessons learned document to the project completion report. Both reports should be stored in the database with all the other project documents. This report includes

- Name of project manager;
- Project team members;
- Project results summary;

> – Include sponsor and stakeholders' acceptance and satisfaction with deliverables, achieving project benefits and success at meeting quality and/or performance targets.

- Project successes (positive outcomes).

The optional deliverables can offer additional useful information. With the project manager feedback, you request information on your performance as a project leader from your sponsor/stakeholders, team members, customers, vendors, etc. You can use this information to further develop your skills to become a better leader, communicator and builder of high-performing teams. Below is an example of what the feedback form could include along with a rating scale of 1–5 (where 1 = strongly agree and 5 = strongly disagree).

The Project Manager Feedback Form

- Facilitated project scope, objectives, and constraints were clearly defined during the planning session;
- Facilitated team identification of project activities and dependencies;
- Communicated to the team how the project was going to be managed and identified standards the team would use;
- Obtained sponsor and key stakeholders approval on scope;
- Regularly communicated project status;
- Effectively managed issues, project risks, and scope changes;
- Involved the team in documenting lessons learned; and
- Write in: Provide comments on project manager's leadership.

Also optional is the feedback form for team members. Team members may request to receive feedback from the project manager and other team members. Some examples of what the feedback form should include are the following with a rating scale of 1–5.

The Team Member Feedback Form

(Rate on a scale of 1–5, where 1 = strongly agree and 5 = strongly disagree.)

- Understood the project scope, objectives, and constraints;
- Identified activities and their dependencies and took ownership of activities;
- Provided realistic activity duration estimates;
- Contributed to schedule compression and schedule adjustments, as needed;
- Took responsibility for completing the activities they owned;
- Reported activity status to the project manager in a timely manner;
- Informed the project manager of new activities, issues, or problems; and
- Contributed to documenting lessons learned.

Step 3: Communicate Project Close

The required deliverable is

- communication

The optional deliverable is

- Compare projects

You are now ready to communicate the project is completed and closed to

- Sponsors/stakeholders;
- Clients, vendors if applicable;
- Team members; and
- Others as needed.

The format of communicating the project close include a meeting, one-on-one, email, WebEx, or any method that is appropriate to close the project. The information that should be communicated is

- Project is closed as of date;
- Summary of the project;
- Location and address of database where information can be found:
  - Scope
  - Project status reports
  - Sponsor/stakeholder updates
  - Risk register and risk worksheet
  - Change requests
  - Lessons learned
  - Project close document
  - Costs of project
  - All other documentation

The optional but recommended deliverable is to compare projects using the report function. The project manager may want to run a compare projects report. In the tracking software you are using, it is very useful to run a compare projects report. This report shows changes in the current project compared to other projects, along with other useful information.

Step 4: Project Closed

The required deliverable is

- Archive project

The optional deliverable is

- Celebrate

The project is now completed and ready to be archived. All the documentation has been placed in the database, the project has been closed in the project software, and the close of the project has been communicated. Conduct one last review of all the documentation to make sure the project information is complete. Finally, archive the project plan according to your organization's guidelines. Review the project close checklist to make sure you have completed all the deliverables.

Sample Checklist: Celebrating Success (Project Close)

Completed	Steps	Activity
Yes	1	Organized and archived all project documentation
Yes	1–4	Successfully led the project
Yes	2	Conducted project close
Yes	2	Involved the team in documenting lessons learned for the project
Yes	3	Communicated project close
Yes	4	Project closed

Congratulation to you and your team. Celebrate all the accomplishments together. The celebration is one more way to continue building team loyalty. It is also beneficial to reflect on the project and review all your successes and anything you want to do differently. To conduct this reflection, you can review the best practices document and the project checklist. Congratulate yourself on a job well done and begin promoting yourself and enhancing your career. Make sure your supervisor and other leaders are informed about your many successes.

Accelerating Your Career

WHAT AN ACCOMPLISHMENT! You built a foundation for success, created a high-performing team, delivered the business goals leading to project success, and celebrated success with your team. You should now be able to see yourself as the amazing person you are and your future potential, which is only limited by your internal beliefs. You have incredible potential to pursue the life of your dreams. This chapter will provide additional information on how you can increase your opportunities in project management and beyond.

A gap exists between skilled project leaders and the availability of professionals to fill the need. Consequently, there is great opportunity in project management with a very positive job outlook for project professionals. Let's begin by looking at how to continually develop leadership skills, the focus of this book.

Leadership

To move forward in your career as a project leader or in other areas, sound leadership skills are necessary. It is understood that a project leader understands technical project management components. However, leadership skills significantly increase successful project delivery. Everyone can become a leader. Let's look at what successful leaders do.

Successful Leaders

- *Focus on attitude.* Your team always knows what you think of them. How do you interact with them? Do you include them in the planning process, utilize their expertise, and help them expand their skills? Do they feel their work is respected and acknowledged? Have you communicated that you trust them to solve problems on their own and make decisions for themselves without coming to you for every solution? Do you verbally recognize their achievements, listen respectfully to what they have to say, or do you cut them off because you know better? Your words and behavior toward your team significantly impact their thoughts and attitudes. Your attitude causes feelings and actions in your team, and this in turn causes results. Consequently, your attitude including behavior and words is much more important than technical skills or knowledge.

- *Follow project management processes but focus on leading the team.* Following project processes and systems provide a roadmap, standardization, and consistency for the project. It is the leadership provided by the project leader that helps overcome the challenges and helps the team successfully deliver a project.

- *Lead the project team to success.* The project leader has a winning mind-set. In a successful project the entire team is successful and recognized for their contributions. Teamwork is based on trust and joint problem solving. Not all projects will be successful because of multiple reasons external to the team, including reorganization, market changes, technology changes, etc. In these situations, recognize the team as successful.

- *Lead the project as a business.* As the project leader, you need an understanding of the organization and how to work effectively within the culture and show leadership and judgement to address the risks and issues that arise.

David's Story—An Innovation Project Leader

David was assigned a large, complex project to establish a system to identify a process to manage the legacy tools at his organization, a multinational company. The organization had been working on this project for ten years but with no progress because of all the competing interests across departments and countries and the large project team consisting of hundreds of team members. The company upgraded their technology frequently during those ten years. Shortly after David started working at the company, the leadership identified a strong need for a workable strategy.

David was assigned the project. He decided to change the entire approach and work with a streamlined team. He partnered with the sponsor and explained his vision of how he thought the project should be managed. He felt it would be more successful by selecting a small core team and consolidating the decision making to four key team members, each with the necessary expertise and leadership representing one of four major areas that would be represented by a core team member.

Once the sponsor was on board, David and the sponsor selected the leadership team. The responsibilities of this four-member team was to plan the project and identify team members who would identify and complete activities and tasks, activity owners, and activity duration.

The team was identified and met to plan the project. David had prepared for their questions and answered their concerns. They remained skeptical but decided to follow David's leadership. The team planned the project and identified risks and the risk mitigation process, the communication plan, and other decisions. The core team worked well together, became fully involved and enthusiastic. They decided to break the project into three projects in order to give the larger team a feeling of accomplishment. When challenges arose, the team worked together to resolve them. In two instances, they asked the sponsor to intervene and remove the barriers. The project was managed as a business initiative.

David clearly communicated his vision and was able to articulate it clearly to the team, customers, and stakeholders. To the amazement of the core team members, the first project was completed in three months, with the remaining two projects completed within one year. All three projects of the multiphase project were completed in one year. The project team was amazed at what they had accomplished. Because of the success, they worked even harder, receiving much recognition and accolades.

After the project ended successfully, the team members all wanted to work exclusively with David on other large projects. Although fairly new to the organization, David was clearly viewed as a future leader with much potential. He was placed in a group of high-potential employees to be assigned a mentor to help prepare him for additional responsibilities.

If you are looking for an excellent leadership course, you can paste the link in your browser for this leadership program at the C-Fame Academy: http://bit.ly/cfame-special. You will receive a special discount. This course will help you

- Demonstrate your leadership skills to the sponsor, stakeholders, and your team;
- Create focused, productive teams;
- Find amazing opportunities that you never thought possible; and
- Create wealth for you and your family.

Communication

In addition to leadership, a second essential skill for project leaders is good communication. Good communicators are good listeners who are skilled at reading the group and their moods. They are able to read the environment well and adjust their messaging to its needs. They are good at responding to the needs and expectations of the team. Let's look at a few qualities of a good communicator.

Good communicators

- *Are concise and clear.* They think through the message they want to communicate and spend time preparing to present it in the best way possible. It is always better to be clear and concise in your communications so people walk away understanding the message, what is expected of them, and actions required. A rambling, disjoined communication leaves everyone confused and results in everyone having a different understanding of the message. It requires much more thought and preparation to be clear and concise. Brevity and clarity help you build a high-performing, motivated team and highly satisfied sponsors, stakeholders, and customers. The project leader needs to be clear in his or her own mind on the message in order to communicate it effectively to others. A good example is providing a one-page status report to your sponsor that has all the information needed.

- *Have an open mind.* Be open to dialog with team members who express different ideas to better understand their position. The ability to openly discuss these ideas often creates a more productive and engaged project team. Become a good listener. A meaningful dialog supports the team members in committing to the success of the project. Let your team know you are always open to new and innovative ways to handle situations. An example may be a very young, inexperienced team member who identifies a new and different approach to a technical problem. Do you have a negative, kneejerk reaction to new ideas that challenge the way things have always been done, or are you open to working it through to do something much better?

- *Are responsive to the needs of the team.* If you focus on the project team's wants, needs, and desire, you will learn more and be far better informed on the status of the project. Good things happen when you communicate with empathy and caring rather than arrogance. Communication that is authentic and transparent, with no hidden agendas helps turn anger into respect and doubt into trust. Trust and respect are essential components of a high-performing team. Working together cooperatively in difficult, challenging situations where you all pull together helps build respect and trust.

David's Story—Excellence in Communication

David has just been assigned an existing project, during which the project is executed and tasks completed. Due to health issues, the previous project leader had to leave abruptly and took a leave of absence to recover.

The project was in the division responsible for defined benefits plans. The division had just purchased training software for employees and their clients on the use of the benefit plans. The purpose of the project was to install the software in the United States and five other countries, develop a plan to train employees how to use it, and develop a plan on how to have clients use the software so it was intuitive and seamless to them.

David began by communicating with the entire team that he was the assigned project manager and that he would continue to work closely with everyone to make the project a success. He scheduled regular status meetings with the sponsor. He met weekly with the project team to review risks and the mitigation plan, and he developed a more comprehensive communication plan to ensure everyone was always informed and up-to-date on the status of the project. He developed a website with the project information that was accessible to the entire team. He developed a website for employees and one for clients to keep them updated and as a forum to ask questions. He communicated weekly with employees in multiple ways and responded to questions within twenty-four hours. He spent 80 percent of his time communicating and talking to the sponsor, stakeholders, team members, and clients.

It was a large project with teams that included technology, culture for each country, change management, client-focused needs, employee-focused needs, and the training department. The teams worked well together, and he was the glue that kept everyone focused. New software had to be installed at sites within each country. He communicated the schedule to each country and explained the process. He found it best if the team worked with one country at a time to install the software and resolve any difficulties. The training schedule and processes were updated regularly and shared with employees and clients.

The end result was the smooth implementation of the software. The training was a success. Two years after implementation, the company underwent major reorganization and decided to bring in different training software. The project was so successful that the new project essentially followed the same project plan that had been used originally. David's focus on communication was one of the main reasons the project was successful.

Career

You are interested in project management and want to know the best way to prepare. There are different career paths to project management, including a degree, certification, and job experience. Below are a few ways to become a project professional.

- *Become certified.* In the United States, the project management profession (PMP) certification or PgMP are the standard, while in Europe and Canada PRINCE2 is the standard. Many listings for positions include these certifications as requirements.
- *Gain experience.* In addition to certifications, on-the-job experience is equally important. It is the combination of certification and successful experience that increase your chances of advancement. Ask to shadow a project leader or volunteer to join a project.
- *Use business language.* Discuss the value and progress of the project business language (such as ROI), along with traditional project terms (such as scope, schedule, etc.). You will advance more quickly if you use the same language as the leaders who will promote you.
- *Be flexible.* Only use appropriate project management processes and tools for projects. Apply the right mix of project tools. Be flexible on the use of specific methodology.

- *Become the go-to authority for project management.* By taking on challenging assignments you gain visibility, and by successful completion of projects, you are viewed as a leader. Do not blame others when you encounter challenges that occur in all projects. You will be viewed as a problem solver with the ability to move the business forward despite obstacles.

- *Work cooperatively with others.* Always treat people with professionalism, courtesy, respect, and consideration even when there are differences. Build a network as you move forward in your career. Again, as mentioned in chapter 2, your attitude is essential for success.

- *Identify your career goals.* If you are clear about your career goals, you can communicate them to your supervisor, peers, coworkers, and mentor. This will allow you to work closely with your supervisor to accomplish your goals. You will then have a greater chance to be selected for the right opportunity to advance your career. What are you passionate and enthusiastic about?

David's Manager's (Anne) Story—Advancing Her Career

In college, Anne pursued a degree in technology with the goal of becoming a programmer when she graduated. She loves technology. After graduation, she found a job in a large organization as an entry-level programmer. She loved her job, excelled at it, and was promoted every year for the first four years.

One day, her manager called Anne into his office and told her he had a new opportunity for her. The company was considering bringing in new technology and had decided to conduct a project to identify which of the various options would best meet the organization's needs. Anne was asked to lead the project because she had the technical expertise, although not the project management experience. Her manager told her she could work with the organization's project office, and they could help her through the learning process. Anne accepted and worked closely with the project office, and at the end of the project, the organization was extremely pleased with the software that had been selected.

Anne found she loved project management. She decided to become certified as a project management profession (PMP certification) and started attending professional development classes at the project management institute (PMI) close to her office. Her organization paid for the classes. She received her certification and continued working as a project leader, which she loved. She continued to be promoted and today is a director. She is respected by both her leadership and her staff.

Now is the time to use your infinite potential and share your leadership with the world. Celebrate the leader in you by living an amazing life!

About the Auhor

Jane Bryan and her family reside in Chicago. Jane has worked in leadership positions with amazing companies and people for over twenty years. With a PhD in organizational psychology from Illinois Institute of Technology, 1990, she has managed international projects, including a software launch in seven countries with hundreds of team members in US, Asia, and Europe. She is a certified executive coach and Six Sigma Green Belt certified.

Printed in the United States
By Bookmasters